"Gothic Tales"

"Gothic Tales"
By
Fritz O'Skennick

Front Cover Picture
By
Adam Foreman
With Photo Editing
By
Jayde Antonin

Back Cover Artwork
By
Julian "Tin-Head" Johnson

Dedicated to Shaun & Romana

Thank you to my Mum & Dad for all their support and thank you also to Will for suggestions & encouragement…

And another HUGE thank you to Jayde, Adam & Tin-Head for creating the cover pictures & for their continuing tolerance, support & encouragement with all my wacky projects…

And indeed thank you to you, the reader without whom this book would not be possible…

Contents

Foreword

You have been taken from your place in the living world, a spectral spectator to the creatures of the nights and wraiths that bleed from the shadows beyond the veil of humanity... I bid you welcome to **Fritz O'Skennick's "Gothic Tales"**

"Gothic Tales" is a dark collection of the ever popular supernatural poetry as told with the startling clarity and profound depth that many have come to love in the unique style of dark writer and poet, **Fritz O'Skennick.** Now for the first time in one volume, Gothic Tales past, present and previously unpublished collide in a thrilling, chilling anthology.

This collection features tales of vampires, werewolves, ghost stories, demons, angels, aliens, murder, madness, immortality and various other themes based in the science fiction and fantasy genre.

Now in celebration of Fritz's 40th birthday comes this often requested, definitive collection *(definitive to the time of publication)* of dark, Gothic poetry that many have come to love via books, performance and postings on popular poetry site, Allpoetry.com.

Fritz O'Skennick is an accomplished creative artist and writer with many strings to his bow. As a singer, songwriter, poet, novelist, playwright, actor & performer, he has enjoyed varying successes with a number of his projects.

Previously published, some of his lighter work has appeared in various anthologies with other poets as produced by United Press.

His solo debut into literary publication was **"Touching the Darkness"** a highly anticipated anthology of his dark poetry that concentrates solely on his darker work that many have come to enjoy via Allpoetry.com and via performances throughout Wales and parts of England.

His second book **"Fear the Reaper"** is a unique, intense, first-person psychological crime thriller that tells a schizophrenic tale of love, loss, revenge and madness.

This was quickly followed by his third book **"The Darkness Verses The Light"** which is a mixed genre collection of poetry, prose and short stories.

His fourth book **"Who is John Doe?"** is a unique supernatural drama based on his popular stage show of the same name.

His fifth book **"Of Darkness and Light"** is a collection of poetry and prose, featuring new work and also many outstanding collaborative works with fellow poets from all over the World, including a collaboration that features no less than 40 poets in 1 poem as orchestrated and edited by Fritz.

His sixth book **"Dark Confessions"** is an intense serial killer novella and concentrates on the darker nature of man, exploring the facets and mind states of murder, revenge and the lengths we'd go to in the name of love, honor and redemption...

His debut album **"UNspokeN"** (music) was released on Petrified Records in 2005 amidst a string of impressive reviews and radio play all over the world.

Playwright and acting credits include **"It could Happen to You"** and **"Who is John Doe?"** as produced by the former theatre company "Progress Cymru".

He is presently working on a second album of his music **"UNbrokeN",** his new book **"Just the Lyrics"** and writing his new series of sci-fi books **"Temporal Medium"**.

For further details of his poetry go to
http://allpoetry.com/Fritz%20O%20skennick

For further details of his music go to
http://www.myspace.com/fracturedpersona

For further details of his performance poetry go to
http://www.myspace.com/fritzo39skennick

Ghosts & other Undead things… (Rhyme)

<u>Danse Macabre...</u>

Putrid flesh on brittle bones,
decayed to moonlight's gaze.
Immortal troupe living death,
that dance til end of days.
Growing numbers, town to town,
forever walk the Earth.
Til judgement day shall come to pass,
with rictus smiles of mirth.

Tireless, beatless hearts of glee,
in endless Terpsichore.
Souls so lost in bodies spent,
that dance forevermore.
Beware if you should glimpse them pass,
before the rising dawn.
Fore they shall claim you as their own,
a lifeless heart so drawn.

Your soul shall join the symphony,
entrance your soul perchance.
Athanasia's endless night,
becomes Macabre's dance.
Beware the twilight melody,
and lock your windows tight.
Bolt your door and close your eyes,
til morning bleeds from night.
For only when they've passed you by,
you sleep and dare to dream,
beyond the troupe's, dancing dead,
and Death's dark, cold regime.

Sleep well, kiddies…

Bound by the Reaper's Hand...

Light is fading, vision blurs,
alas, my time to fall.
Behold, my heart does beat its last,
and so the Reaper calls.
With final breath, embracing death,
my time has come to pass,
my soul doth rise from flesh and bone,
so free without its mass.

So much that I would wish to do,
to live beyond this day,
I'd right the wrongs, I've done in life
with words I've yet to say.
The Reaper stands before me now,
he's heard it all before,
from every soul that's ever lived,
who've begged for life and more.

'Your life is over, walk with me,
accept of this, your fate,
it's time to leave it all behind,
embrace what now awaits.
Time to leave regret behind,
without you, life goes on.
Friends will mourn and weep for you,
and toast you when you're gone.'

Please, I beg you, spare my soul,
there's much that I must do.
The things I've always put on hold,
and never got 'round to.
I need to be at peace with life
and mend the broken ties,
watch the sunrise with my love,
and gaze into her eyes.

'Why are you so different then,
from those who came before?
I've taken souls throughout all time,
from sickness, age and war.
Why should I extend your life,
appease your soul's ador?
There's nothing I could want from you,
and that's your fatal flaw.'

I hear the voices of the dead,
I hear their heartened pleas.
They walk in limbo all alone,
with wants they must appease.
They walk unseen by living eyes,
enraged by what's denied,
the chance to put their souls at peace
and so from you they hide.

I could help them find that peace
and bring them to your hand,
ease their fear of what's to come
and help their spirit's stand.
You've asked me to explain myself,
you asked what I could do,
well this is it, it's all I've got,
the choice is up to you.

'A tempting offer, I agree,
bring those who slip my gaze.
Would you gladly serve this role,
to live throughout your days?
You'd join the ranks of other souls,
that walk upon this path.
But beware if you betray,
I'll come for you in wrath.'

Thank you, you have my word…

Death and Denial.

The castle walls loomed high above,
Foreboding shadows lie.
Echoes fill the empty halls,
Where ancient spirits pry.

My footsteps ring out loud and true,
My breath before my face.
A shiver travels up my spine,
My heart begins to race.

Upon the wall, I see a man,
Cast blue by moonlit sky.
He beckons me to come to him,
From battlements on high.

I take the stone steps two by two,
To greet this waiting man.
Transparent in the moonlit haze,
And so his speech began.

'Why do you walk these halls by night?
A shadow man expired.
Your journey ended long ago,
Your body long retired.

I've come to help you rest in peace'
He said with hand on heart.
'It saddens me to see a soul,
Too tortured to depart.'

'You're wrong' I said 'its you who's dead,
I see through where you stand.'
He shook his head and then he said,
'I know, please understand.

The choice is yours, believe or not,
For you now to decide.
Walk these halls forevermore,
Or face the fact you died.'

Within my heart, his words rang true,
Shot down in war, I fell.
Have I walked these halls so long?
Denying death so well?

I take his hand to bring me peace,
Embrace what I deny.
So blind was I, for far too long,
I bid this world goodbye.

<u>Lest We Forget.</u>

We walked along the forest path,
dry leaves fell at our feet.
So lost were we upon that day,
in Autumn's cooling heat.

The sun peeped through the browning trees,
a breeze as cold as death.
The shadows danced upon the wind,
like Winter's waking breath.

We huddled close and on we trod,
the wind hard at our back.
To push us on along the path,
with strength our limbs did lack.

Then suddenly our limbs were free,
we toppled to the ground.
We see ahead a battle waged,
an ancient war unbound.

With swords they fight, these armored men,
to death and then beyond.
A battle fought forever more,
poor tortured souls, be gone.

'Remember us, forsake us not,
or lest we be forgotten.
To fight this battle evermore,
for lands and sons begotten.'

The voices fade, the wind is gone,
once more the trees are still.
The Autumn day regains its hold,
by Nature's force of will.

A hole is formed where battle raged,
with armored bones therein.
Confirming doubts of sanity,
that fought to rise within

What did we see that Autumn day?
An ancient savage war?
Did we put those souls to rest?
At peace forever more?

Remember now, the deeds of men,
some born of Evil grown
Can never rest a victim's soul,
until the truth is known.

The Ship of the Damned...

So many, many bygone years,
from port a ship didst sail,
a galleon of broken dreams
that breached beyond the veil.
A crew whose souls were cursed that day
to sail forever more,
to never feel their beating hearts
or walk upon the shore.

But every year to mark the day,
at docks the ship is seen
to read the hearts and minds of men,
dark souls with deeds unclean.
A phantom fog and putrid stench,
a shift, a breach in time,
ragged sails on rotten bough
and coated decks of grime.

Behold the Ghost ship, 'there she blows',
by moonlight, harvest comes,
to press gang souls of ill intent
who hear the ancient drums.
They come because it summons them,
with sins that leave no choice,
bespelled as if by siren's song,
a fight that has no voice.

And so they join the weary crew
of putrid flesh and bone
to sail the seas forever more,
a life they dost atone.
So beware the sound of drums
and fog upon the sea,
if thou art less than pure of heart,
the ship shalt come for thee.

A Prosopopeia of Decay

The Reaper comes to one and all,
behold his touch, your time to fall.
For I shall follow in his wake,
a thankless task I undertake.
For you shall take your final breath,
and lay your body down in death.
Vacant eyes that know no more,
so pale now in the face you wore.
Only Death can lead me here,
take your soul and end your fear.
Leave me do what I must do,
dispose of what remains of you.
My tender kiss to corpse so fresh,
induces decomposing flesh.
My touch shall bring your atrophy,
beheld in growing entropy.

Rigor mortis sets its course,
pooling blood with no remorse.
Congealing in a carcass cold,
stiffened limbs as rot takes hold.
My sweet caress shall putrefy,
as host to Death's soft lullaby.
Worms and bugs and maggots feed,
fulfil their part as Death decreed.
All succumb to mortal fate,
from birth to grave and so I wait.
And as the wheel of life shall turn,
in hopes that those who die return.

But all just fade to dust and bone,
beneath the earth and marker stone.
Its what I do in Death's ballet,
its who I am, I am decay.

The Corpse like Bride....

She rises from the grave by night,
her rage and hate unfed.
Unfairly killed upon that day,
when vows and thoughts were read.
To him she gave her heart and soul,
and he returned in kind,
a brutal deed so cold of will.
How could she be so blind?

So now a year has passed since then,
a year unto the day.
And so she seeks him out once more,
for vengeance come what may.
Woman scorned, hear her roar,
make the night her own.
For when she finds her killer groom,
bestow the rage she's grown.

Senses tingle, eyes of black,
and so she feels him near.
He'll rue the day he took her life,
her thoughts and will are clear.
She finds him sleeping out the night,
in lavish room throughout.
Bought with silver left by her,
so now there is no doubt.

She drags him screaming from his bed,
'Behold your corpse like bride.
Did you think I'd leave you be?
A year since whence I died'
He humbled in her haunting glare,
his eyes red rimmed with tears.
Confused she sees that love is there,
consuming all his fears.

'Take my life, my corpse like bride,
your death was not my will,
without you here, I cannot live,
of grief, I've had my fill…
You tripped and fell and banged your head,
and so your death ensued.
Take me with you, please my love,
to live in death renewed.'

Her eyes are full of tears now,
as hate and rage subside.
Could she really be so wrong,
about the night she died?
She takes his hand and leads him free,
his body dead and still.
And so they walk in blissful death,
the bride and groom fulfilled…

Madness and Ghouls and Ghosts, Oh My
or alternatively
"Time to Chew Boom-Stick...Baby..."

I hear the shadowed voices cry
as darkness calls to me.
I see the dead all rise and walk
with pleas that I will see.
The ghouls who feed on dying flesh,
unseen by light of day.
Possessing living hosts to feed
with skins in moist decay.

Should I act on what I see
and kill these living dead?
The only real fear I have,
is its all in my head.
I sit here with my shotgun raised
and hold them in my sight,
feeding on a fresh young corpse
beneath a moonlit night.

They strip the flesh from tender bones
and savor its sapor.
Jagged teeth that tear through meat
with relish, craving more.
An eyeball plucked from socket deep
and slurped between the lips
and popped by closing jaw so ripe
as fingers crunch like chips.

A graveyard full of empty graves,
devoured of flesh and bone.
Am I the only one who sees
them move from stone to stone?
I need to be so very sure
that what I see is real,
but lately things are not quite right,
I don't know what to feel.

The ghosts don't like their corpses ate
and taunt me now to shoot.
They beg me be the hand of fate
in ghost and ghoul dispute.
To sacrifice a living host
that they may rest in peace,
assuring me that even ghouls
will find a sweet release.

A ghoul looks up to see me there,
he grins and charges near.
And so I have to make a choice,
at once my path is clear.
I close my eyes and squeeze them tight,
my finger on the trigger.
I lightly pull as shot booms out,
my heart beats with such rigor.

Reverting to his human form,
his eyes they question why?
His ghost it stands before me now,
he didn't want to die.
Suddenly I'm set upon,
the ghouls they hold me still.
Reverting to their human form,
so shocked they'd seen me kill.

Everything becomes a blur,
a blow that leaves me dazed.
When I wake I find myself
confused and slightly crazed.
A strait jacket that binds me tight
and padded walls and floors.
The thing that freaks me out the most,
this room it has no doors.

Days go by and Doctors come
but nothing's as it seems.
Night time brings the voices call
while plagued by ghoulish dreams.
'I know I have to save the world,
for none see what I see.
I know I must get out of here
but none would set me free.'

'For now, I'll have to bide my time'
I grin so lost in thought,
'and wait until the time is right,
when ghoul fiends can be sought.'
Distantly a voice calls out
and faces all surround.
*'Nurse, I think we're losing him,
make sure he's tightly bound'*

*'10 c.c's of Lithium,
lets hope that does the trick,
that's the third time he's got out,
watch him, he's very quick'*
I rock so gently back and for
as meds invade my dreams
and lock me in my own dark world,
where life's not what it seems.

Ghosts & other Undead things…

(Freeverse)

Dark Clarity...

Death's cold caress
numbs my senses.
He wipeth away
my tears lovingly
and sings
a soothing lullaby
in the silence.
The dead surround me,
plague me, pursue me.
I look for thee,
But thou dost not
walk among them.
Where fore art thou,
My love?

I listen for thee,
amidst a sea of souls.
I feel thee,
yet thou art so very far away,
beached by darker tides.
I yearn for thee,
but I fear thou art lost to me.
Divine realisation
Stabs at me
with sudden clarity.
Fore I know
that I belong
in neither world.
Yet, I exist in both.

What am I to do?

<u>Resident Evil...</u>

Oppressive cold spots,
all throughout my home,
filling me with fear & dread.
Flickering lights, footsteps on the stairs,
knocking my door all hours of the night.
Only to find there's nobody there…
He's coming, I feel him watching,
waiting, biding his time…

Whispered voices in the darkness
as I try to sleep, laughter jarring me awake.
Dark visions fill my mind unbidden,
making me question my very sanity…
Tears fill my tired eyes,
I wrap my pillow around my head,
covering my ears to this madness…
Why won't it stop?

Possessions moving around,
going missing, getting knocked over,
static charging the air.
A breeze as cold as death, passing through me,
yet no doors or windows are open…
His presence is felt
and so my friends no longer call.
Why is this happening to me?

He's growing, getting stronger,
feeding on my despair.
His pungent stench fills my nostrils,
as his darkness fills my mind.
He likes my bedroom and has made it his own,
forcing me out, banishing me
to the living room and the waiting sofa.
And so I sleep in foetal night terrors.

I awaken, breath like steam before my face,
hands and feet like ice. 'This is ridiculous'.
And so unto the bedroom I go
to confront my resident evil…
Each step getting heavier and more painful,
as a blanket of dark foreboding
and oppression washes over me,
consuming me, engulfing me…

Tears stream down my face,
but I fearfully stand my ground.
'This is my home, get out and leave me alone'
He laughs at me, attacks me,
jabbing me across my ribs, back and arms,
forcing me, pushing me out of the bedroom.
Bruises quickly follow and I know it is futile.
And so I sleep on the sofa
'til I've saved enough money to move out.

Never to return…

And So the Dead Shall Walk the Earth...

Sepulchral shadows bleed
from the spectral darkness
of the cold, stone crypt,
forlorn in its neglect,
yet so alive
as malefic whispers
shroud the lifeless corpse
of this vile fiend
in a euphony
of necrotic animus.

So ambrosial
are the archaic voices,
rising to a sonorous chant
in the forbidden verses,
stirring the carrion
from its putrid decay,
becoming the pivot
that ruptures reality
to form a gateway
to the great beyond.

Such malice emanates
from the void,
bestowing to the umbrage,
unimaginable wraiths
of unmentionable evil,
veiled since
the dawn of creation
and once more,
the world is tainted
by their ubiquity.

The mort draws breath
and arises
with a rasping gasp,
a vixen of composing beauty,
her eyes vacant,
her composure insentient,
her skin deathly pallid
as she twitches and jerks
like one dressing in flesh
for the first time.

She climbs the stone steps,
each footfall
steadier than the last,
each breath
deeper in it's taking,
stepping boldly
into the moonlight
with an unnatural grace,
almost animated in a
distorted parody of life.

She rests a palm
on the old apple tree
that adorns the necropolis,
smiling as she reaches
for the forbidden fruit,
grasping it
and defiantly biting into it
in recreation of the first sin.

She smiles to herself
as the dead leave their crypts
all across the churchyard.
'And so it begins,
Humanity holds
not a sliver of hope,
fore they will be but fodder
to the flames of Apocalypse'

The Afterlife Testament of Sir Francis Knollys

Walls in ruins,
battlements unarmed,
so much has been lost
to time and memory
Once my home,
where I walked these dark halls
with majesty and purpose,
lord of my castle,
king of my dominion,
master of all I beheld.

1568, such a sectarian time,
the sisters of regency,
caught twix't faith and blood,
lost to honour and pride
that waged fear and hate,
dividing a land in belief
Wary of scary Mary,
captive by order of the crown,
unseen as Beth rises
to the throne of England
as the syphilitic King
lies cold in the earth,
a tyrant
that spawned two queens,
deadlocked
in a sibling rivalry
of such deadly apportionment.

Did I do right by my country?
Did I do all that I could do?
Alas, I fear not, lest why else
would I be forever destined
to walk these castle halls
amidst the phantoms
and spectres
of purgatory's hand,
a mere apparition
forsaken of death's
sublime embrace,
a simple curiosity
that chills the minds
and souls of living hearts…

Please forgive me…

Twixt Penance and Rage...

Why do I bind myself here?
Such turbulent thoughts
that plague my tortured soul,
bringing the madness upon me,
bestowing such euphoria
and despair in equal abundance,
blanketing my broken mind
in such sublime darkness,
consuming me in its fluidity,
killing me softly,
in its ethereal essence.
And I couldn't crave it more…

Sleeplessly I succumb to the night,
walking among the dead,
singing a soft insomniatic lullaby,
tranquil beneath a melancholy moon
that bathes blue my nocturnal reverie.
They caress my lifeless flesh, so tenderly,
so lovingly, yet oh so cold,
like a penitent lover,
pliant in her betrayal
wearing her piteous lies
like cerements to her corpse,
longing for a peace that will never come.

And so here she lies, inanimate,
abed in a haven of foreboding,
desolate to my indifference,
bestowed an eternity of woe,
lost to an ocean of sorrows,
suckled to my crimson rage,
forever to lie in purgatory, a slave to her duplicity.
And I, her keeper, her redeemer who never shall redeem.
My corpse long cold by my hand,
bequeathed of a Judas-kiss.

Twix't Blood & Dust...

Crossing Worlds,
walking among the dead,
shrouded in a
blanket of night.
Restless, they call,
no longer seen
by living eyes,
but for chosen few

A gift that has its curse,
a madness,
concealing a truth,
holding me captive
in its relentless onslaught

Transcending
perceived reality,
bound to causal nexus,
smoothing ripples
in actuality,
holding entropy at bay
Voices calling,
Angels falling,
caught twix't
blood and dust
in an ocean
of divine darkness…

An instrument of destiny,
a prophet scribing whispers,
lost to my purpose,
seeking a sign
that brings clarity
of fate's will

Hast thou forsaken me?

Final Curtain...

And so I take my final bow,
my lines complete,
my role at an end,
discarding my mask
like a true soubrette,
leaving the stage,
to sit in the wings,
hiding from the light
as the show goes on without me.

No more my heart
may beat to passion's tide
as breath exhales its last
and blood congeals
in the Winter of life's
closing juncture,
concluding the book
of existence in a chapter
of reminiscence and regret.

Forever watching,
always listening,
no longer bound by sleep,
invisible to the eyes
of the living soul,
but for chosen few
who see beyond the veneer
of corporeality's
sublime paramnesia.
But alas, I learn more
of life in death
of humanity's nature
than in all my years
of mortal cognizance.

And I realize, how strange the living feel…

The Curse of the Shadow Man...

She stands in the sublime darkness
of the ancient dank cellar,
ancestral home to a lineage
that spans the centuries,
shrouded in the mystery
and dark magicks of familial bonds.
'Adeo mihi, meus atrum procur'
she whispers unto the umbrage,
breath before her face,
hands clasped in anticipation as she awaits his return.

He bleeds from the penumbra
atop the antediluvian stone steps,
casting a watchful if not lustful eye
upon the crimson clad beauty
that awaits his advent,
a Shadow Man bound to servitude
for age old transgressions,
bespelled under aegis
of the Warlock's hand,
impelled to eternal vassalage
of the alchemist's bloodline,
'til love finds him humbled
to serve by his own will.

So long has he waited,
a prisoner in his own mind,
lost to the motions of peonage,
yearning a freedom
that's price defies his nature,
unknowing as his heart skips a beat
at the sight of his current mistress
and he obeys her whims
without question or intrinsic contention,
that his subjugation has long since passed...

'Ego sum hic , meus era...'

...Wraith...

...Thump, thump...
...Thump, thump...

...Heartbeat slowing...

...No, no, no...
...It cannot end like this...
...I have so much more to do...

...Thump, thump...
...Thump, thump...

...Pulse weak...

...So very cold...
...I don't want to go...
...I WILL NOT GO...

...Thump, thump...
...Thump, thump...

...Numbing cramps...

...ARRRRGH...
...Damn it, do you hear me???
...I... WILL... NOT... GO...

...Thump, thump...
...Thump...

...Clenched teeth...

...Holding on...
...Mind over matter...
...WILL RESOLUTE...

...Thump, thump...

...Light fading...

...Darkness falls...
...Still... I... am... Here...
...Holding back the lambent passage...

...Thump...

...Breathing fails...

...Stay away from the light...
...I... DEFY... YOU...
...Be gone... I fear thee not...

... ...

...Free of the flesh...

...Time is the enemy...
...Flesh, its weapon of irony...
...It strikes me down...
Yet...

...STILL... I... RISE...

...

In Death We Dream...

Such dreams that lie
beyond the veil,
an irony in reflection
of a life lived
that all may walk a path
so restless in the regrets
of all that came before.

In life, I craved
such peace
as quietus bestows,
a happy ever after
whispered
in a twilight berceuse
that I may lay me down
to eternal slumber.

But alas it holds
such empty promise
in the falsehoods
beheld in an
inquisition of pain
that lie beyond
the voices that descant
the silence
of corporeal lullabies.

In death, I dream of life,
specters of all
that I have ever held dear,
mirrors of all
that I would change,
an echo of the forgotten,
phantasms
that cantillate sentience
in the shadows of light.

I cry for my loss of self,
I mourn
the mundane moments
in the beating
of my heart,
such events
that would fair take
my breath
and race
my blood to soar.

I look upon
my pale carrion,
so cold, so still,
sweetly soothed
in decay's gentle caress,
an illusion of peace
to reassure the living
in hopes of tomorrow,
beliefs formed
to appease
the sinful hearts.

All succumb
to Reaper's kiss,
so painless
in its passing,
yet few can find peace
in the choices made
and walk unburdened
into the light
and so we sit
in purgatory's hand…

…Waiting…

Clawing the Casket Lid...

Eyes snap open

...Darkness...

'I can't see... Where am I?'

ANXIETY!!!

Head moves, seeking

...Cramped...

'Arrrgh!!! Banged my fucking head...'

CONFUSION!!!

Hands smoothing velvet

...Crepuscule...

'Phone!!! I've got my phone...'

HOPE!!!
Fingers forage pockets

...Confined...

'Low battery???
You've got to be fucking kidding me...'

ANGER!!!

Jaw drops open

…Screen light…

'I'm in a box… A coffin?'

ALARM!!!

Body tenses sharply

…Constrained…

'FUCK! FUCK! FUCK!
I've been buried alive…'

PANIC!!!

Bloodied, broken fingernails clawing lid

…Tenebrosity…

'Think, think, think… I have to think…'

CLAUSTROPHOBIA!!!

Breathing getting tighter

…Encumbered…

'The air is running out… I'm in the ground…'

FEAR!!!

Heart thumping against ribcage

…Calignosity…

'I'm not going to make it…'

DREAD!!!

Breaths hampered, erratic

…Stymied…

'IT… CAN'T… END… LIKE… THIS…'

TERROR!!!

Heart slams shut, choke

… …

'Sighhhhhhhhhhhhhh……..'

Vampires & Werewolves...
(Rhyme)

Ageless Hunger.

I walk among you mortal men,
the ages pass me by.
From blood soaked hands, to war strewn lands,
I feed on those who die.
Before they take their final breath,
the blood still warm inside.
To feed my raging hunger pangs,
before the shell has died.

It saddens me to see a world,
where such as I may roam.
With memories of ancient days,
to far to call my home.
I live and breathe by twilight shades,
I walk denied by all.
My skin no more shall know the sun,
until my time to fall.

My soul is torn, for those who mourn,
the souls who wait for death.
They feed me life, and end their strife,
until their final breath.
To justify this way of life,
a balance must be drawn.
Perceive ye mortal cattle men,
and bless the souls, I mourn.

So when its time to judge my sins,
of life and lust partaken.
I know inside, when life's denied,
my soul shall be forsaken.

Prince Charming.

I travel through the countryside,
on steed, I'm riding tall.
As black as night, my steed in flight,
I'm drawn as voices call.

'Please come to me, my one true love,
behold my body still.
With skin so cold, yet never old,
thy prophecy fulfilled.

Just one kiss to bring me life,
and end this wicked curse.'
Who is this girl before my eyes?
Who speaks these words in verse?

Her skin so pale, the air so stale,
a corpse in twilight glade.
Is it wrong to lust and long,
for dead girls flesh displayed?

I kneel beside my corpse like bride,
and kiss her lips so cold.
Her opened eyes find mine and pry,
as life for her takes hold.

A feral smile of malice born,
distorts her beauty fair.
Her eyes as dark as blackest night,
revealed in moonlight's glare.

She bites my flesh, my senses numb,
my heart pounds in my head.
Consume my soul within my shell,
dispel this passing dread.

So now I breathe my final breath,
she holds me in her arms.
Hunt with me, my one true love,
embrace these sinful charms.

She takes my hand and leads me free,
a bloodlust fills my mind.
And so we feed throughout the land,
unknown by all mankind.

<u>Choices and Siredom...</u>

Beware these ancient eyes beheld,
a heart as black as night,
for I shall be all things to you
that make your world seem right.

I'll make you feel the deepest love,
I'll fill your soul with bliss,
I'll rise your passions deep inside,
and all with but a kiss.

They call me creature of the night,
a demon without soul,
who feeds upon the purest blood
for strength to make me whole.

I feed upon your innocence,
entice your soul to sin,
in death, I'll make you drink of me
to feel me deep within.

So wait until tonight my dear,
beneath the moonlight's gaze,
for I would sire you from life,
and ease your soul's malaise.

I'd lead you through my twilight world,
embrace the night we'd own,
to leave behind your darkest fears,
beyond this life you've known.

For I shall never lie to you,
of who I am I show,
so very few are worthy of
this gift that I bestow.

I offer immortality,
I offer you the night,
I offer you eternal youth
that comes with but a bite.

Now think upon the things I've said,
the price of this, your soul,
the sun no more may touch your skin,
but I would make you whole.

For now I take my leave of you,
or burn in rising dawn,
so choose if you would wish to be
my child of night reborn.

Lycanthropy.

Why does the moon affect me so,
when full in darkened sky.
A searing pain inside my brain,
a blackout time is nigh.

Bones are cracking, limbs deform,
my voice becomes a growl.
The pain I feel is all too real,
my cry becomes a howl.

A rage inside and lust for blood,
beneath the moonlight's gaze.
The world blacks out, I know no more,
until the dawning rays.

I wake up naked and confused,
my nails are caked with blood.
Metallic taste within my mouth,
I'm sick into the mud.

Where have I woken up today?
a park or maybe zoo?
This sickness seems to rule my life,
I don't know what to do.

A flash of blood, a tear of flesh,
disjointed in my mind.
Am I mad? Or do I change?
This beast and I entwined.

With wolfsbain shots and silver cross,
I prey unto my lord.
Spare my soul, this sickness curse,
and evil spirits ward.

The time has come to choose the way,
to end this evil curse.
Silver bullet through my mind.
so ends this tragic verse.

The victim souls of killings past,
can rest by what's in store.
For when they lay me down to rest,
my soul shall know no more.

Vampires & Werewolves…
(Freeverse)

I Wouldst Sire Thee, My Love...

Please, be not afraid,
for all my faults,
I really am most agreeable,
Ah, I dost see that I hast amused thee,
thou doth presume me arrogant,
that an ancient creature
such as I wouldst dare to postulate
that I couldst maketh thee anxious.

Thou really art most beautiful, my dear
and dare I say it, so very brave.
That thou couldst return'eth
in light of that which wouldst
be so awful to thine eyes.
Prithey tell my lady,
Couldst thou find forgiveness
in thy broken heart for this soul
that wouldst be so very black to thee?

Couldst thou forego an eternity
of bitter pathos and sate
thy boiling rage in dreams
of better futurities?
Time is fleeting,
lifetimes so brief in their passing,
shining bright afore they snuff
to eternal darkness,
eclipsed in a twilight ballet
of amaranthine chimeras.

I offer thee immortality, my love
for thou art so very far from average.
Thy bluster so breezy
as to beguile my heart,
enchant mine eyes,
bespell my soul.
Thou dost walk a bumpy path,
so broad yet so long
with such vitality
and allure that thou doth
stir my passions so…

I beseech thee
in my adoration of thee…
I wouldst sire thee…

What sayeth thee, dear lady?

__Immortal Yearning...__

I am such a fool,
so eager was I to embrace my immortality.
That not once did I consider
how very long eternity can truly be.
With just one bloodied kiss,
she seduced me to the darkness.
I sacrificed my soul to her charms,
a willing lamb to the slaughter.
Sired in blood,
awoken from death in adulation.

Naked, shaking, confused.
Temples pounding,
searing birth pains,
raging hunger.
And so she laughed,
mindful of her own siring.
She beckoned me to her.
'Come my love, feed with me.'
she whispered softly,
biting into my flesh.

I tensed in suppressed euphoria,
before finally succumbing
to guilty pleasures
and fading inhibitions.
I bit into her, drank deeply
and fucked her with a passion
I have never before known.
Such perfection,
such ravenous beauty,
such bloodlust…

And so the hunt began,
the scent on the wind,
the fear in their eyes,
the lust in our souls.
Oh the games we played,
Stalked, cornered, terrified.
The heartbeat of prey,
forfeiting life in it's betrayal to my ears.
Sweet life blood seasoned with fear.
Oh how we fed…

We made bitter sweet love
in the falling ashes of Pompeii.
We kissed without abandon
as Rome burned and perished.
I held her in my arms
at the fall of Arcadia,
with a love so all consuming
and never ending.
We walked in eternity
with a passion transcending the ages.

For a millennia,
we slept in the shadows.
Unseen, unknown, forsaken.
Feeding in the velvet darkness
on the flesh of the lost and weary.
We watched as nations rose,
We fed as civilizations fell.
Growing ever bolder
in our twilight playground.
Gods among mortal men…

But alas, all must finally perish.
All must turn to dust
and try as they may
to find peace in eternal slumber.
I lost her… my beloved dark angel…
Impaled as she slept
by hunters of our kind.
She shrieked a curdling, fearful death cry,
and I awoke with a terror unsurpassed
since I was mortal.

I leapt into the air with great lustre,
ripping apart the nearest to me.
I bellowed my rage at them,
swatting arrows out of the air
with a focused agility unknown to me.
They scattered and fled into the night,
my rage unfed, my thoughts in flux.
I held her in my arms, weeping
as she looked into my eyes
one final time.

'I shalt live again, my love… find me '
she whispered softly
and crumbled to dust in my arms.
I shrieked my raging sorrow
into the darkness.
I ran into the night,
their scent still fresh in my nostrils.
My vengeance was unmatched
by any before me.
Such carnage, such cruelty, such gluttony.

I sired their children,
I raped their women,
I fed them to their heirs.
And so their village burned
from time and memory
in a wake of blood and fire.
None lived to recant my fury,
none lived to regret their transgressions.
Even the sired children perished
in the rays of the rising dawn.

Yet despite the justice
of my dark fury,
I found I was unable to draw satisfaction
or solace from my brutal vengeance.
Without her, I'm an empty, hollow shell,
heartbroken and alone,
without purpose or reason.
And so I slept,
untouched by eternity
as the decades came and centuries passed.

Awoken only by a mournful lullaby
that heralds to my soul
that she walks this Earth once more.
Yearning, stirring, awakened.
I rise with purpose,
shaking off the murky shackles
of deepest slumber.
Ravenous, I feed and brave this new world,
searching, craving, tasting her very essence
on the edge of darkest perception.

Fear thee not my love, fore soon I shalt be with thee once more…

Immortal Yearning II The last Vampyre...

Hiding in the shadows unseen,
feeding in a world beyond my perceptions...
Changed beyond my recognition...
Have I truly slept so long?
I stand, an echo of bygone days...
An industrial revolution? An age of reason?
My kind, no more... A simple fiction
to scare children in their beds...
A lineage claimed by extinction
in the foot notes of eternity...

Our proud nobility, our ageless heritage...
Gone... Siphoned to hearsay...
Retold by charlatans and fools,
ridiculed beyond redemption
in a cold, sparse world,
lacking chivalry and honour...
Time has not been kind to humanity,
fore they have lost their hearts...
A new sorrow chills me to my soul,
I'm the last... I'm truly alone...

I need you more than ever, my love...
You must rejoin me, lead me, through
this harsh, sterile new world that has lost its way...
I must find you, awaken you, sire you...
That we may walk in eternity once more
with a love that transcends the ages...
I feel you, I crave you, I need you...
You tease my perceptions...
You stir my soul...
You awaken my heart...

By moonlight I search for you,
growing ever closer as I feel your presence
grow ever stronger in my mind…
Projecting my essence to your dream states,
that I may awaken your soul
in recognition of your immortality…
Do you feel me?
Do you yearn for me?
Do you remember me?
So much has been lost to time…

And so lost have I become…
Seasons pass in a parody of life,
The birth of Spring, the youth of Summer,
The age of Autumn and the death of Winter…
And so I search for you, immune to its cycle,
A relic of Athanasia's twilight ballet…
I feel you, you begin to reach out to me,
Calling me, beckoning me to you,
Like a siren's song to this weary traveller…
'Come to me, my sweet Lucius , Find me, my love…'

She calls me by name! What diabolism is this?
My Lady, Aelia calls me by name!!!
By the Gods, it is spurious that a mortal
should hold such power… To call out a Vampyre?
To call out a Vampyre of past life cognizance?
What game have the fates conspired?
Frustrated, I must find cover,
Lest I be charred in aurora's glare…
Clock is ticking… Thoughts are racing…
Soon, I shalt be with thee, my love…

I found such shelter as to be lorn in its neglect,
full of the most dire wretches that my eyes
have ever beheld,
huddled like vermin to the nest…
They did not even glance at my approach,
but for one piteous knave…
'Smack, I need smack' So smack him I did
and fed from his cullion jugular…
Too late I taste of the venin tainting his blood,
decending to my knees in alchemic delirium…

I awoke latterly, my prey long cold,
his consorts indifferent to his quietus…
Is life so paltry here,
that none would mourn his passing?
This is not my world…
I fear humanity without its heart
become the monsters and demons more so than I…
It was their benevolence and compassion
that made them rich in their pedigree
and savoured in their sapor…

At eventide I leave in search of Aelia,
she calls to me once more, so close now…
Soon I shall hold her in my arms
and nevermore be sorrowed to solo pursuits…
It has been so very long, loneliness my only companion,
her rebirth, my yearned utopia…
Such was the time of her passing that I craved my end,
that my long slumber be eternal,
disturbed only by hunters of our kind,
to be blissfully lost to Reaper's kiss…

But alas, fate brings such kismet happenstance,
that decrees the circle be complete…
That I may sire she who bestowed this life upon me…
Give to her the gift she gave to me, immortality…
She calls to me, no longer in my head,
but on the night air, but a walk away…
Such joy in my heart as I've not felt in five hundred years…
She is returned to me…
My dark Angel, my love… My everything…
With tears in my eyes I run to her and her to me…

We embrace, we kiss, we are lost to the moment…
She wipes the tears from my eyes…
'My poor, sweet Lucius, you find me at last…
Walk with me my love, let us share this night,
let us share ourselves, let the circle be complete…'
She leads me to her home… She laughs, music to my ears…
It amuses her greatly that she must invite me in
before I can cross her threshold…
She does, so soon are we lost to our passions
in a manner befitting our immortal hearts…

As one, we quake in frenzied peak,
holding each other tightly as she sits astride me…
'I love you, Lucius… Remember that'
'Always' I smile 'As I love you' Tears well up in her eyes,
I move to comfort her and feel the spike of the wood
slide up under my ribcage 'Forgive me, my love…'
'Why?' my startled eyes plead, she holds me in her arms…
'Our time has passed, I'm setting you free'
She holds me tightly and sobs…
'You are a nobleman out of your time, sweet Lucius'

'You will live again as have I, my love'
I smile through crumbling lips at fates irony,
I smile at the beauty and the poetry of it all
as the unforeseen circle completes…
She who brought me into this life, takes me out of it…
There is no betrayal, I love her more than ever…
Freed by lasting love transcending lifetimes…
I reach out to stroke her cheek one final time
as my hand flakes to dust…
There is no pain, only peace and the chance to live anew…

Fare thee well my love…

Hell Hath No Fury...

In the dark enchanted forest,
grim shadows danced and played
as the sun peeped through the trees
onto an old worn path that led
to the embittered hag's abode.

From a tender young age,
she'd been a fair child,
raised by her stepmother,
upon the death of her father,
rest his soul,
killed in the jaws of a giant wolf
that roamed the woodland,
she'd sworn that day,
that she would have its hide.

For many years she dabbled
In the dark arts,
donning the cloak of the witch
chanting from a spell book,
with many mishaps along the way,
turning her stepbrother
into a stout troll
and her stepsister into a hen
but she never gave up

One dark Winter's night
as snow blanketed the land,
carried on ill wind from the east,
a peasant graced her doorstep,
seeking shelter for the night,
a handsome fellow indeed,
poor of wealth, but a heart of gold.

She quickly ushered him inside,
sitting him before the hearth
and stoked the embers to flame
'Aye, ye are a kind lassie, to be sure'
the last word rolling off his tongue
in a burr that made her heart flutter.

A passion rose in her
like she had never felt before
'Could this be love?' she wondered
'Oh wooer of woman-folk,
my name is Lily West and prithey tell sir,
what is thy name?' she asked bashfully,
offering him an apple,
in a manner befitting Eve's
first temptation in Eden.
'My name is Ranulf Lyall'
He fixed her with a predatory grin
and bit heartily into the apple.

Days turned to weeks,
weeks turned to months,
and soon, Winter passed to spring,
Lilly lovingly tended house
as Ranulf hunted by night,
they were betrothed,
they were so in love.
She thanked the Heavens
that they should bestow
such blessing upon her

Until one fateful night,
A mighty howl echoed
through the woodland valley,
freezing the blood in her veins,
fear gripping the pit of her stomach
into uneasy knots of dread.
Dear sweet Ranulf
was hunting this night,
that alone, gave her strength,
as her horror grew to rage

The wicked beast would not
take another she loved,
she held her spell book to her heart,
uttering an incantation of protection
and ran into the night
'Show thyself, beast, I fear thee not'
The giant wolf dropped
on its haunches before her,
its sinewy brawn taut,
beneath the gaze of the full moon.

But it did not leap,
it simply padded a circle
and lay before her.
'What art thou waiting for, brute?
doth thou toy with me?
Hast thou not tormented me enough?
Fight me...'
She kicked it hard in the ribs and
it winced through sorrowful eyes
'Nay, Lassie, I wish thee no harm'
it growled. 'Forgive me, my love'
'Ranulf?' she took a step back...
'Aye Lassie, it is I'

'You killed my father?' she wept.
'I was new, the beast was all consuming,
I had no control, I was lost to its blood lust,
t'was my wish that I may right the wrong
I hath bestowed upon thee,
if thou wouldst wish my hide
then I shalt fight thee not'
Her mind reeled at the implications
of his words, tears stinging her cheeks.
'I shalt not kill thee, my love' she sobbed,
taking a step towards him

'Step back from the beast, miss'
a desperate voice cried.
Suddenly, numerous musket shots rang out,
echoing throughout the land.
The wolf yelped and writhed
amidst the onslaught of bullets,
his blood soaking into the soil around him
as villagers came into view,
muskets raised as they approached
'No... no... Ranulf???' she knelt at his side
her tears falling like Autumn rain.

His bones cracked and his skin
retracted fur, as his face
became familiar in the features
she had so grown to love.
He reached up and stroked her cheek
'Always know, I truly adored thee, my love'
he uttered with his dying breath
and was lost to quietus.
She roared a racking cry
as a hand touched her shoulder.
'Its over now, miss' said the proud villager.
'Over... OVER??? Thou hast made me a widow Sir'

Her irises flashed red as she stood,
forming a dark aura around her,
storm clouds quickly gathered
in a rage filled night sky.
The ground quaked and villagers ran in fear
as she rose into the air above them,
a true mistress of the dark arts,
wrath shimmering off her in waves.
Lightning cracked, smiting villagers in its wake
and so she grinned,
fully embracing the darkness of her fury.

Many years have since passed
in the dark enchanted forest,
And still, the grim shadows dance and play
as the sun peeps through the trees
onto the old worn path that leads
to the embittered hag's abode.

Devils, Demons & Angels...
(Rhyme)

I Sold My Soul for Chicken Wings!

Torrential rain and blackened sky, the day I sold my soul.
Foreboding dark and lightening strike, as thunder starts to roll.
I stand beheld by shadows dark, a train that never comes.
Well this is great, my train is late, my feet and toes are numb.
Rumble, grumble, gurgle, roar, the hunger pains are back.
I didn't have a chance to eat, the food and drink I lack.
I'd kill to eat a scabby horse, or eat the scraps thrown out.
I'd sell my soul for chicken wings, just meat with bones cut out.

Behold a man in red and black, a smile upon his face.
He beckons me to talk with him, a soul so far from grace.
He held before me contract type, and quill that drips blood red.
'Just sign here, and here, and here, and so you shall be fed'.
I signed the form in triplicate, anticipate my feast.
Saliva dribbled down my chin, my hunger pains increased.
A bucket full of chicken wings appeared before my eyes.
Just meat and skin, no bones within, a smell you can't deny.

'Be seeing you', so said the man, 'my business here is done'.
He faded in a puff of smoke, but laughing 'cause he'd won.
So many different chicken wings, some spicy, plain and sweet.
I gorge myself in greasy joy, a tasty, costly treat.
I sold my soul for chicken wings, the best I've ever tried.
The memories of that costly treat, will haunt me 'til i've died.
And then beyond, the Devil's due, my soul for wings was bought.
Damnation for eternity, no solice can be sought.

How stupid we, as mortal men, can be in weakened state.
I sold my soul for chicken wings, for me it is too late.
Heed my words, behold my tale, eternal soul be burned.
So weak was I to chicken wings, a lesson must be learned.

The Hero's Grave.

Looking at the tombstones, of those who've lived and died.
Thinking of their funerals, the people who have cried.
What was it like in their day, was there one like me.
Looking at the tombstones, thinking life is short but free.

All the stones are big and wrote, all of them but one.
Its small and partly buried, it's a shadow in the sun.
The boy he was a pauper boy, a hero live and dead.
Who sacrificed himself for them, for a bullet in the head.

Looking back the years in time, to see what happened then.
Satan risen up from Hell, and taking souls of men.
This boy he was a fighter, a hero sent from God.
The power of good upon his side, and light shone where he trod.

He set off on his journey, to face the Devil's wrath.
The darkness came and shrieked its rage, as Satan broke his path.
A rain of fire did scorch the land, his shield his faith in good.
The seas did boil and blood run cold, yet still our hero stood.

The boy brings forth his book of faith, and quotes in Hebrew verse.
And banishes the Evil one, to end this wicked curse.
Demons screech and Angels cry, the boy fulfils his quest.
But Satan's parting gift to him, ensures he'll never rest.

Possessed by Demons raging hate, oh fragile mortal mind.
He begs his fellow men to end, his pain bestowed unkind.
They kiss his cheek, perform last rights, with tears in their eyes.
A gun shot echoes through the land, and so our hero dies.

Hell's Prophecy...

Words foretold in print so bold,
Events have come to pass.
Deeds of men from now and then,
Displayed in mirror's glass.
Demons wait and feed the hate,
Ignite the flames of rage.
Mans decline, defined in signs,
As words upon the page.

Passing through the nexus view,
As barriers doth fade.
Oh so strong, the demon's song,
As innocence is slayed.
Man may fight eternal night,
Alas, his plight is sown.
Born to sin beneath his skin,
A demon army grown.

Crawling flesh of sins so fresh,
Immortal souls be burned.
Now they pray to quell the day,
The demons have returned.
So sublime, the end of time,
Can man change his ways?
From the sin so deep within,
Before his final days.

Beneath the Harvest Moon...

I fell beneath a harvest moon,
Cast out of Heaven's grace.
To walk this Earth, a mortal man,
Alone without a trace.
I sit beneath a starless sky,
The blood moon fills my view,
Heralding my banishment
From endless life I knew.

I sit and ponder for a while,
The Angels raging war.
Endless in its ageless squall,
The rights of man, its core
Men have souls and we have not,
They're favoured in his eyes,
Made them in his image bold,
And we, the slaves to lies.

Fight in light for all thats right,
This fallen Angel sings.
Eternal life, a fading dream,
These bleeding stumps, my wings.
To now become a human male,
And feel this aching soul.
The fears and hates of mortal men,
A gift that has its toll

Death can come at any time,
For fragile mortal man.
Deep inside I feel alone,
A first since time began.
Was it worth the sacrifice,
Now death can come so soon.
So many thoughts I ponder now,
Beneath my harvest moon...

Behold the Demon...

I am the Darkness in the night,
the Demon in your mind.
I am the thoughts you try to fight,
that make your will so blind
I whisper to the hearts of men,
entice their souls to sin.
And so my voice calls out again,
and claws so deep within.

I tell you things that weaken you,
the lusts that you abhor.
I make you hate the things you do,
yet make you crave for more.
Convincing you, you have no choice,
that this is who you are.
Become the slave unto my voice,
I'll see you fall so far.

Projecting thoughts into your dreams,
embraced as are your own.
'Til in your eyes, the madness gleams,
beyond the lusts you've known.
And so you act on my command,
my joy to watch you fall.
Corrupted soul with sin so grand,
beheld within my thrall.

Eternal Darkness is my face,
depraving souls of man.
With all the souls that fall from grace,
I've lived since time began.
You see me in the rage unfurled,
my will shall not desist.
My greatest trick upon your world,
you think I don't exist.....

Possessed...

I saw the Demons boldly rise,
from flames within the pyre.
Clawing from the depths of Hell,
baptized within the fire.

Laying claim to all the souls,
who walk this world in sin.
Corrupting hearts so pure and good,
by twisting faith within.

Taking form in weakened hosts,
as vessels of their will.
Bringing on the end of days
in deeds of ageless skill.

I fear I hear their voices call,
frenetic host, so numb.
Fighting darkness in my mind,
I pray I don't succumb.

Shadowed thoughts so deep and dark,
in many tongues they speak.
Blacking out my faith in light
and making me so weak.

Writing of their thoughts and schemes
in fictions to amuse.
Read these words and heed them well,
behold their timeless ruse.

For when they come, the test is faith,
to hold their will at bay.
Strong the heart who keeps his soul
in faith, so come what may.

Devils, Demons & Angels...
(Freeverse)

Cleansing Nights

Damn this decrepit frame,
so frail and pallid…
I can't even look at myself
in the mirror anymore…
Why do I always let it
come to this?
Suppurating poisons
from diseased flesh
in grim anticipation
of my immortality…

Such is the power
of my hoodoo,
jongmans, deficient
in moral purpose…
A chalice of blood,
Hair, an image, my intended…
Maniacal by moonlight,
I whisper 'inruil'
Brittle boundry broken,
restoring my youth anew…

A Requiem of Angels...

You are the light to my darkness,
The calm to my storm,
The hope to my despair…
I adore you,
I crave you,
I need you…

Embrace this fallen Angel
And let not the heavens,
Sate our passions…
Hold me,
Kiss me,
Love me…

You reflect me in desire,
You mirror me in thought,
You share my abilities…
Dream of me,
Feel me,
Touch me…

I knew you would come,
Tear my world asunder,
Bring me to my knees…
Awaken my soul,
Enflame my heart
Stir my passions…

Long have we walked this path,
Destinies entwined by fate,
Convergance unseen...
Always waiting,
Never knowing,
Ever lonely...

I walked in the darkness,
Amidst the dead and the dying,
Broken to my purpose…
You found me,
You held me,
You saved me…

Now I can't live without you…

Fighting Destiny's Hand...

How could I be so wrong?
I was so sure…
I should just
surrender to fate,
stop grasping for light
in the darkness
of destiny's design…
I'm tired of fighting
who I'm meant to be…
Stop losing myself
to impossible dreams
to distract from
the inevitability
of becoming host
to the demon…

I so want to be good,
pure of heart and soul…
But always he dwells
within me,
blanketing my soul
in darkness,
consuming me,
suffocating me…
How much of my flesh
must I cut?
Before my shell
is scarred
beyond destiny's hand?

I don't want to be
the destroyer…
I don't want to be
the bringer of darkness…
I don't want to be
the harbinger of the end…
I don't want to be evil,
nor hear the voices of the dead…
I don't want
to harvest the living…
I don't want
to manipulate their thoughts
or occupy their minds
in preparation
of prophetic dreams…

Sweet blissful quietus,
my yearned for friend…
Oh how I crave you…
Yet I fear the demon
would pursue me
to purgatory,
wrenching me back,
forsaking my heart
in its possession
of my soul…
I am so lost…
Every choice,
a step on the path
of Shaol's divine plan…
I'm so afraid
to let loose inhibition
in fear of the demon's grasp
on my mind…

I wish humanity
wasn't so fickle
and shallow of heart
as to let the darkness
corrupt them so easily,
leaving me less
to hold onto…
Walking a lifetime in slumber,
awakened to despair,
fighting my nature
in avoidance
of becoming the beast…
All paths lead me here
and so I weep,
lost to divine dark purpose…

The false prophet falls,
the fallen angel
is forsaken,
lost to
the demon host,
the seal is broken,
the gates of Hell
dehiscent,
darkness taking flesh,
cleansing the world
in a blanket of flame
and so fate comes to pass…

Release me Micah, show me a different path…
Please…

Twilight Carnival...

Fog quickly blankets the ground,
music carrying through the trees,
a haunting, mournful piper,
beckoning the lost and forsaken...

Fore they will come, curious,
seeking shelter, seeking warmth,
seeking distraction from fear,
befallen of stature and grace...

They will laugh, they will cry,
They will gasp, they will applaud,
and all it will cost them is their soul,
laments quelled before they are sonant...

Behold the trickster, dark inamorata,
fore tonight, she is the raven beauty,
an ill omen to all bespelled of her gaze,
tonight, she sates their hearts desire...

Shiver, prickling flesh... A lost child?
Innocence with heedless enchantment,
a morsel of the most ambrosial kind...
She seeks, she stalks, she feeds...

Fulfilled of animus, savoured sin,
and quoth she nevermore...
The show goes on, for but one night,
a harvest of desolate élan vital...

Welcome to the Twilight Carnival,
what is your pleasure, sir?

Fallen Angel...

Falling from
Heaven's
Grace…
Cast out…
Bestowed
with a soul…
Immortality
fading…
Wings burnt
to stumps
in a dark
toxic sky…

Falling…

Free will
was all
I craved…
Independence
of thought,
to make
my own choices,
unbound
of God's hand…
I have my wish
but I fear
the price
was too high…

Falling…

PAIN!!!
I've never…
Felt that before…
Sensations…
Unknown to me…

It hurts…
Oh God
help me…
It hurts
so much…
I am
so scared…
For the
first time,
in all
eternity,
I know fear…

Falling…

Humanity
washes
over me…
I am unclean…
Unworthy…
Stripped
of my
servitude,
lost
on the path…
No more
may I walk
in the light…
This is
not what
I wanted…
Yet…
It is all
that I
asked for…

Forgive me Father, for I have sinned…

Harbinger...

She is the calm before the storm,
the eye of the hurricane,
the bringer of chaos,
where she walks,
destruction reigns
in abundant ataxia,
a trail of carnage
catenates
in her wake.

She is vengeance,
she is rage, she is envy,
she is the harbinger
of wanton madness,
she brings delirium
to the hearts of men,
tainting the fragile balance
of sanity's grasp,
lifting the veil of lucidity,
unleashing the beast,
devouring the souls
of devout hypocrisies.

Beware the bird of prey,
fore he shall be her eyes,
the omen that heralds
her dark advent,
preceding
bedlam's fury.
And so he waits,
his mistress shrieks
in the flames
of acrimony,
mindful of
prescient whispers
that speak of
approaching quietus
in dreams of Omega.

Yet she welcomes its cold embrace…

<u>The Passion of the Fallen Angel...</u>

Hold me my love…

So long have I yearned
to feel your soft caress,
to be embraced
in your arms
once more…

I have fallen so very far,
I have seen things
that you could
not conceive
in your most
agrarian nightmares…

I have languished
for an eternity
in the pit,
my wings
but stumps
to the rage
of Abaddon's inferno…

I have walked
the world of man,
a stranger
in a strange land,
fearful of their
barbarous ways…

…They know not what they do…

So long have I strived
to be with you,
to hold you,
to touch you...

...To love you…

Even for but a moment
would sate the
raging loneliness
in the vast emptiness
of eternity's bite…

And now I return to you,
my tears, an abundance
of such sorrow
and such joy...

...My heart cries for you...

...For I have changed
so very much…
So dark is the path
that I walk,
lit only in the light
of remembrance
in the torch
that I hold for you…

So long is the road
that led me here,
so much pain,
so much suffering,
so much that
I would wish
to tell you,
my love…

…And I kneel
before you,
an abomination
in the eyes
of all that is good…

…Can you still love me?

Devils, Demons & Angels…
(Prose)

Lucifer's Sojourn...

Where is the justice? Where is the loyalty? Where is the love?
I would gladly bestow my heart in gratitude for a beloved kindness
bequeathed me by my brothers and sisters of the world. Such
simplicity and cooperation in sublime generosity is sacred yet they
would betray me and slander my name without a second thought.
God only knows, I try to be a good man, stand tall, proud of my
honesty and good intentions yet so lost in a ruthless world of
cunning, spineless con artists, highly skilled in the artful finesse of
mendacity.

My wounded soul climbs the heights of Helicon to gaze upon
Helios and Selene, entranced by the darkness and the light that
beckons Euterpe, my muse who brings to me the clarity and poetry
of life. Fore I see the Demon in the eyes of children, hidden in the
diabolic depths, corrupting their souls with such divine purpose, a
traitor to their innocence.
I hear the sweet music on the night air, a violin played with
masterful beauty as to trance me to the core beneath a sullen moon.
So arcane, so brilliant as to bring me to tears and strip me of my
armor in the eyes of this dilettante who shines like a star. His
genius beyond any words that I could castigate of him, his bearing
like that of a king, to possess such honor and authentic self
awareness. He approaches, his rapturous melody coming to an end
as his haunting tones seep into Mother Nature's velvet umbrage.

His eyes shine in the moonlight, shifting color like gems of
alexandrite, piercing with power and an air of plutocracy. Yet his
manner befalls one far more humbled to life's attitude. Like a
polymorph that would engender many faces in disguise to the
expectations of the beholder. And so he joins me in this twilight
liaison. When finally he speaks, his silken voice drips tones of
Mephistophelian seduction as to flatter my senses.
'What troubles you, my friend?'
The familiarity of this stranger should violate all that I hold in truth
yet I find him quite intoxicating and quickly endear him to my soul
and begin to tell him of my woes.

'It is my Father… Today I had news that his health deteriorates beyond the doctrine of the known sciences and his Holiness would have me sit with him 'til quietus takes him. It has become such a huge incubus to me'

'His toil is known to me, it is why I have sort you out'

'Who are you? Illuminati? Royal house? What do you know of me?'

'That is my secret to keep, all you need know is that I am a law unto my own freewill and the demographics of every man, woman and child in this world are known to me' A predatory smile spread across his features but I cared not.

'Why would you seek me out?' I asked desperately as he laid a consoling arm about my shoulder.

'I sense your soul is in jaundice of your beliefs'

'I beg your pardon Sir?' I gasp, open mouthed.

'If I may use an analogy of the stars my friend, like Sirius your soul has split in twain. Sirius A shines brightly in belief and conviction as Sirius B consumes itself in rage and doubt and this is what I believe troubles you so deeply.'

'What am I to do?' I wept as a tear ran down my cheek. He held me by my shoulders and looked deeply into my eyes.

'What if I were to tell you I could expunge your Father's sickness and bring him back to healthiness? Would that bring foundation to your troubled soul?'

'I would say do it… Please… I will pay any price…' Again came his predatory grin.

'And so you shall my friend, consider it done'

He took my hand and shook it hard, causing me to wince as a sharp, stinging pain crossed my palm. I quickly withdrew my hand and looked at my palm to find what looked like a small burn in the shape of a cross. When I looked up, he was gone. 'The man moves faster than a cheetah' I mumbled as I felt water drip off my nose just before the Heavens burst into torrential rain and thunder rumbled across the tenebrous night sky.

And for the first time, I wondered to myself…

'Did I just make a deal with the Devil?'

Death is beneath you...

How far, must an angel fall from grace, before he knows humility. That he may find purpose in his role of divine retribution. Such a sentience should know conscience, that he may weep for the lost souls of decadence and sin. To bring death to the likes of these, must not bring joy, nor must it be savoured. For a higher purpose is to be served. All must know their place in Tribulation, a line must be clearly drawn, separating the light from the darkness. Few would walk between that line, fewer still would wish too. I see the growing entropy, in the darkness beyond physical reality. It slowly rolls along the edges of my peripheral vision, gathering momentum, gathering speed, as it enshrouds the hate, bitterness and jealousies of mortal men. Such is my gift, that I may define the boundaries of good and evil, and know that my will although ruthless is true. There are always choices. And with choice comes consequence. And with consequence comes a responsibility to face up to the choices we make.

Oh, I'm terribly sorry, did I startle you?
You must further forgive me, my intrusion of your personal space.
For I wish to take you on a journey.
You're on a downward spiral going nowhere fast, no hopes, no dreams, no peace of mind.
People nagging, people shagging. Deceit, betrayal, despair.
Who will grieve for the loss of purity and innocence in a world that encourages deception?
Homicide, suicide, genocide, megacide.
Death is beneath you. I'm going to shake your world; I'm going to break down the walls and barriers of self-doubt and delusion.
I'm going to bend your very reality and your perception therein shall crumble your very belief system and all you hold in stone.
I bring order to chaos, I bring light to darkness, I bring hope to despair.
To you, I bring clarity to the mixed emotional confusion of thought and mind, that you may heed my words and follow the right path and know that your destiny is fulfilled.

Man's destiny is beset on all sides by doubt, confusion and temptation.

Man's very nature dictates paranoia, territoriality and greed, and by that measure will he be judged.

Do you not feel that man has lost the right to govern himself? That a new order must come into being?

When you look around, do you not see 'Famine', 'War', 'Pestilence', and 'Death'?

Yes my friend, the Horsemen ride bold in this era of human history. For are these not the last days?

Do you not feel it?

Do you not see it, as you look around you?

As you observe the carnage, injustice and chaos of man's reign.

All over the world, our cities run rife with sin and debauchery.

There will be a reckoning, for the time of tribulation is at hand.

Never in the linear timescale that we call eternity has it been more imperative to seek repentance and pray for our immortal souls.

Tell me my friend; if you were to look death in the face, would you accept his cold embrace in the name of justice?

Or would you turn your head and walk away?

I believe you would face him, for death is beneath you.

Your sense of conscience shall uphold and maintain your integrity, and in humility, you will kneel before the maker.

Autism, schizophrenia, obscessive compulsive disorder, all mental genetic disorders that will be rectified in the new order.

For with the divine creator we must seek redemption and hope he sees forgiveness.

No man is beyond repentance, no man is irredeemable, for also in man's nature is the ability to change.

Is it not so, that the most devout atheist is drawn to prayer in the face of death?

All souls shall be reaped and harvested in the restoration of the forgotten genesis.

The light and the dark shall divide, tilting the balance of power.

Earthquakes, famine, pestilence, drought, and flood. All these signs be!

You must walk this path; you must not deviate or bow to temptation.

You shall seek wisdom and enlightenment, and in doing so, you shall find salvation and understanding.

You must spread the word, so that all shall know the end of days. As it has been foretold, you shall walk this path that I have set out before you, for death is beneath you, and my life is forfeit.

The torch is passed, and my role fulfilled in the coming judgement of man. Now go forth in all your beliefs and prove to me, that I am not mistaken in mine.

Fare thee well my friend, and Godspeed to you.

Science Fiction & Fantasy
(Rhyme)

The Visitor's Dismay...

I come from very far away,
beyond this place in time.
Your world is full of petty hates,
such ignorance and crime.
I woke one day to find I'd slipped,
through cracks in temporal grace.
My horror grew to see you are,
a brutal, savage race.

No compassion, no remorse,
with values gone astray.
How do you live your daily lives?
In fear from day to day?
Obscene, repugnant, selfish, vain,
you judge by what you see.
Race or gender, gay or mad,
all focused targets be.

Poisoned oceans, spoiled lands,
yet still defiling more.
Kill the world in which you live,
for greed and pointless war.
Wasteful, wealthy, bellies full,
while others starve and die.
Ignored, betrayed and pleas unheard,
yet no one questions why.

Cruelty dealt to one and all,
with torture, death and strife.
Coldest hearts are born sublime,
yet no regard for life.
You scare me with your heartless ways,
I watch in sad despair.
I walk among you sadly stooped,
now trapped without a prayer.

Monster.

Upon a rooftop in a storm,
the lightening gave me life.
The gothic towers a beacon to,
my birth by lightening strike.
Convulsive pain, I scream inside,
a man made man unfree.
My birth, a curse upon the earth,
abomination be.

Discarded from the Baron's grace,
I walked the Earth alone.
Despised by man, a monster be,
until my mind had grown.
I learned to read and then to write,
a blind man's deed, so kind.
But still I felt alone inside,
my need for love, a bind.

I then set out to find the man,
who made me what I am.
From bits and bobs of corpses past,
and so my life be damned.
Behold creation at your door,
the man made by your hand.
Denied, he ran from coast to coast,
across the sea and land.

I need a bride or mate for life,
behold my heartened plea.
Deny me not and make me whole,
and then I'll leave you be.
Deny me now and face my wrath,
your life shall be undone.
For I shall take your love from you,
like me, you'll be but one.

So full of pride, he made my bride,
unknown, she should deny.
The kindred soul in such as I,
no matter how I tried.
Enraged I fled, my need unfed
and joined a circus fair.
A Freak Show seen by one and all,
alone without a care.

The decades came and centuries past,
until this modern day.
I now can pass as human stock,
immortal man displayed.
My wounds are healed, my scars are gone,
and so I seek once more.
A mate to walk through life with me,
and face what lies in store.

A dedication & homage to Mary Shelley's "Frankenstein"

The Mirror's Other Side.

I looked into the mirror,
When I was on my own.
My hand went through like water,
How could I have known?
In I put my head to see,
The mirror's other side.
Head first it pulled me in and then,
My senses numbed my pride.

Floating in the darkness,
Memories pass me by.
Drifting in this place that has,
No ground or even sky.
I hear the whispers chant my name,
A breeze as cold as death.
I hear a dripping fill this place,
Consume my every breath.

All around me, windows form,
That only have one side.
People go about their lives,
My presence here denied.
I hear them plot, I see them plan,
I see them brush their hair.
I see them dress, I see them sleep,
Of me they're unaware.

Along this line of mirrored glass,
I drift until to mine.
I see myself inside my room,
A shiver up my spine.
I knock, he sees, he says 'you're back',
And in he thrusts his hand.
He pulls me back into this world,
Alone, I try to stand.

What the Hell! I cry out loud,
Confusion fills my head.
Was it real? Or just a dream?
Of life and thoughts unsaid.
I touch the mirror's surface cold,
To summon back that place.
Nevermore to breach the world,
Beyond the mirror's face.

Taken...

Driving through the lonely night,
'til dawning rays doth shine.
A country road that leads me home,
to warmth and sleep divine.
My company, my radio,
With tunes that sooth my soul.
Until the moment fate steps in,
and dreams of sleep are stole.

First the engine splutters still,
The radio but static.
My compass spinning like a wheel,
my brain on automatic.
What the Hell is going on?
This car is nearly new.
Okay, I drove three hundred miles,
but that's the job I do.

A shadow passing overhead,
so silent in its wake.
And so I step into the road,
with fear that makes me shake.
A burning light doth penetrate,
and hold my body still.
My feet no longer touch the ground,
I'm pulled against my will.

With no control, I float aboard,
   so weightless in the gloom.
Hands that grip me in the dark,
   and lead me to this room.
I find myself on table strapped,
   as naked as when born.
Big black eyes in sockets grey,
   so cold, survey my scorn.

A light so bright, can't close my eyes,
   my mouth is open wide.
As drilling starts on open teeth,
   and slits expose insides.
Helpless to the pain I feel,
   and probes that make me blush.
Nerves so raw to everything,
   that cuts my voice to hush.

Suddenly I scream aloud,
   and waken in my car.
Disjointed memories in my mind,
   no sign of any scars.
So I drive as nightmares fade,
   to home and bed-ward bound.
Uneasy in my train of thought,
   my breath the only sound.

The Legacy of Valhǫllr...

Valhalla, Valhǫllr,
Odin's pride and pain.
The golden tree where Godhood waits
before the Hall of Slain.
The warriors of Asgard fight,
in battle now they fall,
led by Valkyries in death's kiss
to honor Odin's call.

So many tales regaled from life
of battles, wine and song,
of great campaigns where men are made
on paths of war so long.
But heroes are a youthful breed,
who live and die by sword,
who fight for glory, honor bound
in Odin's name they horde.

Bragi, God of poetry,
attests their battle tales,
so sublime beyond their time
in words that tip the scales.
Thunder hears the hammer strike
in honor held of Thor,
to welcome chosen warriors,
who fall in mortal war.

The fallen Einherjar prepare
and aid in what's foretold,
the twilight of the Gods has come,
events and deeds unfold.
Ragnarök, the end of days
that herald ages new,
where men find reason outweighs faith
in all they strive to do.

But none forget Valhalla's name,
where heroes pray to fly
upon the wings of Valkyrie's horse
when battle torn, they die.
Embracing all that's come before,
brave warriors retold,
songs and stories sung aloud,
remembering the bold.

Science Fiction & Fantasy
(Freeverse)

Reality's End...

Reality fades into memory,
decay and entropy.
Outlived by time,
Unseen by paradox,
Unfelt by sentience.

It warps in its death-throws,
twisted and unfulfilled.
It burns in rage,
It seethes in denial,
It screams in defiance.

What manner of sedation is this?
Drained and unrealised.
A vague daydream,
so quickly dismissed
in morphian night terrors.

It weeps for its forgotten genesis,
bound and betrayed,
it writhes in loss,
potential unseen,
stripped of its gift.

It questions...

Why?

Prophet of Paradox...

I stopped the world today…
I held back time
by sheer force of my will
and walked in the breach
between moments.

Unbound of linear chronology,
I slipped through the cracks
in temporal grace,
an anachronism
of Athanasia's design.

There is a darkness coming,
eroding the edges of reality
hiding in the shadows of causality,
immune to the growing entropy
of decaying quintessence.

I have seen things…
Terrible things that defy my senses,
that live between the moments,
distorting my perceptions
as they walk absolved of causal nexus.

Prophetic in delphian dreams,
insecure streams, unfixed points,
forked to secondary reality,
exploring aleatory potentials,
unmaking all that came before.

Time winds howling, ripped apart
turning tides on temporal waves,
lost to wounds that weep and seep
through cracks in actuality,
forever changing all that stays the same.

I am but the messenger of paradox,
an anomaly of the coming storm,
I see the agents of chaos,
I see entire worlds fall in temporal flame,
purged and supplanted by falsehoods.

The Darkness is Coming…

<u>Hyde and Seek...</u>

Days blur,
weeks pass,
months
become seasons,
dying a little more
each year…

Control becomes
an illusion
I hide behind…

Smiling
to an uncaring world
as rigor-mortis
sets in,
numb to my tenure.

When did restraint
begin to elude
my grasp?

When did he begin
to see
through my eyes?

Slipping
through the cracks
of my waking mind…

I felt him coming,
yet I did naught
to discourage him…

When did I give up?
When did he become
so strong?

Waiting in the wings,
wearing me down,
waiting for me to slip…

Is illusion
all I have left?
The pretence that I live,
one foot in reality…

Stood on the threshold
of my downfall…
So lost in my dream…

Hyde is awake!!!

***A dedication & homage to Robert Louis Stevenson's
"The Strange Case of Dr. Jekyll and Mr. Hyde"***

Sibylline Whispers...

Transcendental dreamscapes
ascending the veneer
of perceived actuality,
darkness bleeding
through CRACKS
in the entropy,
eroding the EDGES
of reality...

Losing TIME... Losing SELF...

...Temporal chronology
NO longer linear...

Its nature vacillates,
mutating in ATROPHY,
as memories ally
to delphian DREAMS
as the PATH splits in twain,
then thrice fractured
to pythonic whispers
that FILL the VOID
in visions
that resound and SCREAM
in a MAELSTROM of voices,
HOWLING in a storm of RAGE,
LOST on the WINDS of change
with DIVINE revelations
that are as judicious
as they ARE infelicitous...

The barrier IS failing,
breaking down
as realities BLEED,
merge and weave,
rethreading the tapestry,
HOLDING existence
in the BALANCE,
boldly rising
from the DARK time,
an ECHO of
the forgotten genesis,
rewriting the slate,
UNSEEN, unfelt, unknown
by ALL but those
touched by MADNESS,
BROKEN prophets,
beheld in the EYES
of SUBLIME chaos…

Perceiving the FACES
that GLIMPSE
through the VEIL,
KNOWING untold
of the caller's CHIME,
finding AXIOM
in a STRANGER'S projection,
ATTUNED to the shadows
of restless EIDOLON,
a MADNESS of sanity,
a SHARD of truth,
cocooned in a LIE,
WRAPPED in a blind
psychic psychosis
that FINDS life
in a fragmented MIND
that SEES all…

…Yet STRUGGLES to be WHOLE…

Anxious Musings of the Immortal Mind...

People understandeth not…
How couldst thou fathom
the divine intricacies of eternity
with a mortal?
I hath lived for so very long,
I am forsaken of rememberance
of more than thou
couldst ever know…

Yes… I am immortal…
Do not asketh of me to explain myself,
for quite simply, I cannot.
It wouldst be likened to thee
to tryeth explain
the extent of thine existence
to a crane fly.
In twelve blissful hours,
he shalt live a lifetime
without conceptions
beyond the confines
of his allotted time.

However, I shalt say,
it be not the notion of immortality
that thy literature and fictions
wouldst hath thee believe.
I dost live, I dost love, I doth age
and yet I findeth myself bound
to all manner of mortal wound.

Its just…
When death's hand is upon mine own,
my body returneth to a time of juvenal,
restored of youth and vigor
and so my cycle of life
begineth once more,
cursed by rememberance
of that which shouldst be lost.

I see'eth my loved ones pass
as I dost outlive them…
My children, for I hast fathered many
o'er centuries, live their lives
and turn to dust
'neath trodden soil
in the natural course of time…

None yet inherit my traits of longevity…
Nay, can they offer companionship
in the millennias to come…

Always it hurts,
but one dost learn'eth
to tolerate its bite
in the jaws of eternity.
I hast learned to let go,
remember them with fondness
as they dost go gentle
into that good night.
The circle of life dost
continue unbroken,
except for me…

I hath even seen their fair souls
returneth to me
through the ages.
A smile, a nod, a look,
glimpses of recognition,
quickly dismissed
in forsaken memory.
I wouldst yarely embrace
their hearts in a beat
but for wimpled soul.
For how wouldst thou recant the ages
to one lost to time's passing?

I hast fruitlessly sought
others likened to me,
that walketh in eternity
unbound of Reaper's sway,
but alas there art none…
I hast sought out Judas the betrayer,
for scripture's doctrine dost dictate
he shalt forever walk the Earth
in penance of his treachery.
He walketh not
and I knoweth I am not he.
Methuselah, Tithonus, Vlad Tepes,
all men lost to myth
and Chinese whispers
o'er centuries
in the pages of eternity.

Such cruelty as thou couldst never know,
mine ancient eyes
doth grow weary in the light.
Such sorrow in my heart that sings
a mournful lullaby in a soft, gentle aria,
serenading a symphony of divine darkness
to an overture of eternal pilgrimage
empty to my fading élan vital.
I am so lost... Always looking behind
to find my way forward,
knowing I doth not belong
and I hath lived far too long,
yearning an end that cometh not.

I hast been crucified for heresy,
I hast been burned as a witch,
I hast been victim to many plagues,
wars, murder and suicide,
I hath even passed
to age and frailty many times.
But each time I doth rise
and it begin'eth again,
each time I doth hope
it shalt be the last.

I dost fear that I couldst outlive humanity,
that I shalt see beyond Man's final breath,
when all I know is dust and bone
and life hast come to pass,
I shalt be truly alone...
And what of evolution?
Wouldst I be a curiosity
to Man's successor?
And what of world's end?
When Earth returneth to Sun's abyss
and all I know is no more...
Shalt I be forever dieing?

I am so very, very tired...

Atrum Oraculum...

Beware the coming storm,
the thriving atrophy
that draws ever closer,
growing from the shadows
of time's entropic decay…

The evolving darkness
consumes the fading light
in a divine reckoning
that snuffs the flame
of perception's falsehoods…

The time is almost upon us,
we must prepare the way,
as we behold the shift
of anomalous futurities,
that all may find confluence
in the coming days…

For madness shall find sanity
in evolution of perception,
as sanity finds confusion
in its devout inability
to accept the veil's falling…

And so the walls
will come tumbling down
as rationality lies obsolete
in an extinction of life
as we know it,
adrift on a tide
of fear and confusion
befallen on a lost humanity…

We have strayed from the path,
deceived in an age of reason
that is not what it decrees,
creating a cold,
sterile world
of greed and
impurity justified
in the guise of progress…

And so the nature of man
shall be revealed,
forsaken in the flames
of hypocrisy,
unravelled
as the tapestry burns,
sculpting life
from the ashes
of the past
to build castles
from the stones of change…

...The catalyst of vicissitude is upon us...

...Caveo Obscurum...

<u>Alphabetic Truths...</u>

Anomalies Beheld,
Causality Devastated,
Effervescent Futurities
Growing Haunted
In Jaundiced Knowledge,
Left Metaphorically Numb,
Often Pulped, Quantified,
Rectified, Savagely Torn
Under Vagaries
Wrought Xenomorphic...

...Yesterday's Zenith...

<u>Quarantine...</u>

What did they do to me?

Metalic taste within my mouth…
My skin, so pallid and clammy
with a glistening sheen,
so slimy and glutinous.
My flesh, swollen and plump
as my bones protrude
and elongate in a cohesive distortion
of life that awakens the genes spliced
from primeval dormancy.

I was so naïve…
'A flu shot for a particularly deadly strain'
they'd told me as they'd injected
that vicious poison into my veins,
desecrating all that makes me human.
Smiling as I coughed
and gargled pungent mucous.
Writing notes as my blood coagulated
over putrid appendages that grew
from my damp gelatinous shell
with such tenacious fluidity,
entwining my DNA with primitive strands
lost to the darkness of time.

Feeding me wet, succulent morsels
of rotted brawn to keep
my insatiable craving sated.
Cheering as I outlived the other test subjects,
suckling me to the decay of their blackened corpses,
decomposed in the dank, humid atmosphere
that made them reek
and distort my heinous appetites
to hunger tirelessly for the warm,
saporous piquancy of living flesh... Human flesh…

And so I waited, biding my time,
embracing the patient predator I was to become.
More tests, more putrid meat, more note writing…
They didn't even see it coming, I wanted to laugh
but my physiology had too far changed
to accommodate such a human reaction.
With various new limbs and four rows of teeth,
I lashed out faster than even I had dreamed possible.
I rendered two of them unconscious
and fed upon the third, his pained screams
fading to gasps of air as I bit ravenously
into his ropy sinews,
desiccating his muscle to liquid and pulp.

Klaxons wailed, booted guards
charging into the affray,
no match for my evolution,
I sprayed paralysis poisons from sacs in my jaw
at their approach, securing a food stock
to complete my transformation
and build my strength.
Steel shutters dropped,
evacuation protocols executed…
And so they left me in peace… To grow…
They'll be back when they think me dead,
little knowing,
they should have added hibernative dormancy
to my list of evolutionary traits…

And so I wait…

Paradoxal Pariah…

I walk in the breach
between worlds,
a path of endless
potentialities,
fragile in its instability
to change its nature,
beset by darkness
in mood swings
so destructive
as to burn
the stars
from the skies,
as the agents
of chaos
dance
in the fires
of paradox,
feeding
on the ashes
of causality,
distorting
the balance,
rewriting
the pages
of eternity
from
the blood
of the
forgotten,

ceased
in the
wounds
of temporal flux,
a rip, a fold, a tear
in the fabric of reality,
bleeding new tomorrows,
spawned in illusions of today
in a fabrication of our yesterdays
that grow evermore impossible
to grasp in the shadows
of shifting actuality…

Give me
something
real
to
hold
onto

…Please…

The Depths of Love... (Tanka chain)

The galleon creaks,
Sails cling to mast, waves crash deck
Behold Neptune's rage
Tsunami climbs to dark sky
Eyes wide in imminent end

Destruction rains down
Splintered wood, life washed away
Forsaken of prayer
Tragic, unforeseen, no more
Broken men, face down in brine

Ocean calms to breeze
Behold the mermaid's sweet song
The flick of their tales
Searching sailors gasping air
Taking men as mates to depths

Lost to murky surf
Nevermore to see the sky
Drowning in despair
Kissed of life by selkie's lips
Grant a wish to you she shall

Should you seek her love
and ensnare a mermaids heart
as one forever
with every enchanted kiss
lost to depths, the lands forgot

The Sentinel...

As the planets align
and darkness falls
over the Earth,
so will come
the dawn
of change,
a nexus point
where all that was,
is and will be
flutter on the wings
of anachronistic shadows
beheld in the eyes
of temporal flux...

An anomaly
of dormant potentials
that wait in the echoes
of the uncreated,
whispers of what
could be,
fighting
for existence
in a chorus
of dominion
that chant
in the impact
of shifting tomorrows...

For none can hear the cries
that shriek from the void,
growing in number,
growing in strength,
devouring
the causal nexus
in delphian nightmares
that fade before
the rising dawn,
leaving such
bitter uncertainties
in the supernova souls
of the dreamer's perceptions…

And so as the veil falls,
all shall see what awaits,
all shall know
what is to come
and all shall
see as I do,
but alas they rise
from the depths,
grafting
consciousness
onto a reality
that repels them,
yet weakens
to their onslaught
in the breach
between moments…

Time is running out,
for who shall
watch the watchers
when perception
is blind
and certainty
holds falsehoods,
crushed in the
hand of fate,
distorting as realities
converge
and merge
in the wake
of the
forgotten genesis…

I grow so very weary,
for so long
have I held back
the darkness,
a sentinel
to the entropy
that grows in the
fractured emptiness
of eternity,
holding back
the atrophy
of a world
whose time
should have
ended so very long ago…

Please tell me, I am not the only one…

<u>Temporal Echoes...</u>

Unbound of linear chronology,
an anomaly to causal nexus,
I walk in the breach
between temporal echoes,
a tear in actuality,
an incursion that bends
in a reflection of paradox…

Behold the agents of chaos,
for they rally in the shadows
as realities merge in the eyes
of the uncreated,
fighting for existence
in a world they
cannot comprehend
beyond a veil
of false physicality…

…A moment time-locked, freeze framed...

…Holding back the darkness…

Science Fiction & Fantasy
(Prose)

Nyquil dreams (The call of Avalon)

This fever has weakened me and so in my desperation I drink heartily from the cup of this Nyquil potion. I shiver as icy fingers brush gently along the length of my vertebrae.
So cold... so very cold...
I clutch my pillow to me tightly and draw comfort from its soft familiarity.

Like a petulant child, fists clenched, on my knees, I scream my rage and sorrow unto the void.
Whether by intention, design or blissful ignorance, it mocks and scorns me.
I am enraged by its further unyielding cruelty, knowing my cries shall go unanswered.
Once more I am engulfed in darkness and my very essence is fragmented and scattered unceremoniously on the chill winds of time and memory.
My Demons come for me and I am broken...
Sensing my weakness, they have conspired to usurp me. But which of them would be so bold as to assume that they could take my throne?
Paranoia? Self-loathing? Obsession? All likely suspects I'm sure...

Like foot-soldiers, they gather around me and unsheathe their swords. I raise my head, close my eyes and await the killing blow. Even in sickness, I will not show weakness to them, even if it should cost me my life. I am somewhat relieved as I hear their swords clatter to the stone floor. I risk a peek to assure myself that they are not toying with me and see them all drop to their knees and kneel before me.
'My Liege, I beseech thee. Lead thine army for the glory of Avalon.'
'Avalon?'
'Yes, Majesty. A great Darkness befalls us, that is not of our making'.
'Darkness?'

'Majesty? Art thou bedevilled? Thy words speak confusion, art thy brain addled?'

'No, I have just awokened… up?'

A look of shock and horror pass over his features and he quickly gets to his feet.

'Thou art awake? Then all is lost, Avalon will fall'.

'Wait, it can't be as bad as all that, surely?'

He grips my shoulders and lifts me bodily to my feet, hands shaking in their gauntlets.

'Art thou an imbecile? Doth thou not understand the importance and weight of these events?'

'No I don't. Why don't you explain them to me?' He stares me down, and I stand firm. Testosterone shimmers off us in waves as we each fight for dominance in our rival's eyes. Eventually, he lets me go, sighs and begins his story

'It hath been foretold in prophecy. That one day, the king would wak'eth. And on that day, when his majesty's other worldly soul walks in Avalon, a great darkness would be released and Avalon will fall.'

'Are there no other armies that will help us fight?'

'The spirit folk lack substance and can only observe, although, they do advise wise counsel. The fairy folk art wielding great magics and art prepared to wage cover fire for the advanced guard. The elves will mount an air assault on dragon's wings.'

'Hang on, you're telling me you have dragons here?'

'Do they not sail with glorious majesty through the skies of thy world?'

'What? They breathe fire and everything? How cool is that?'

'I understand not, thy words? I fear thee be fair speaking in tongues were it not for the glimpses of familiarity within. But forgive me, I digress. Surely ye now comprehend that which was lost, and the urgency of our plight?'

'Yes, I do. Is there no more to the prophecy?'

'More?'

'Yeah, like. Oh I don't know, um… the darkness can be defeated by… a swift knee to the happy sack… a clip round the ear and told to bugger off home'.

He took a concealed dagger from within his armour, gripped me, slammed me into a wall and pressed the point into that fleshy fold where your neck meets your chin. I gulped, as he glared at me with barely suppressed fury, his face mere inches from mine.

'Doth thou mock me? I should kill thee where thee stand. I hath bore mine soul to thee, and ye remark with flippancy and disrespect. Thou hast all the guile and cunning of a squashed apricot'

I answered, carefully choosing my next words.

'I apologise most indubitably, I was being facetious and there was no need for it. It won't happen again.'

'Then take care when ye speak, for there are those who would'st not be so forgiving as I.'

He let me go and put away his dagger. The next moment it was like my transgression had never happened.

'We must bare arms and wage battle.' He picked up his sword and held it above his head, the rest of this demon army got up from their still kneeling position, and held their swords aloft also.

'FORE THE GLORY OF AVALON!' he shouted.

'FORE THE GLORY OF AVALON!' they replied.

'WAIT!' I called. They looked back at me puzzled.

'Wait? Time is of the essence and already much is lost. We must away!'

'What do you know of the darkness? Can it be killed? Is it even corporeal?'

'What nonsense doth thou speak now? Corporeal?'

'Are there no wise men, mystics or soothsayers that we can call upon, someone with insight, perhaps?'

'There is a man, a very ancient and powerful sorcerer. It has been said that he was there at the very birth of Avalon. His real name hath been lost to the ages, but he is called by many names. The guardian, the ancient one, the founder...'

'Okay, then shouldn't we seek him out. Surely, he would make a great ally.'

'But he is ancient and we hold many magics.'

'Okay, its your call. But with names like 'the guardian' and 'the founder' I'm surprised no one has sought him out already.'

'Hmm... Thy words hold merit, my friend. But alas, no one has ever sought him out, never thee mind gazed upon him in flesh.'

'But if he's as powerful a sorcerer as you say, maybe, just maybe, we could call him out and he'll hear'

Suddenly we hear a wizened chuckling from the corner of the
room. All eyes turn and the demons draw their swords. With a
wave of his ancient hand, time stops. The demons hold their
swords like a still photo or painting by Giger or Escher. The old
sorcerer strides toward me.

'Finally, someone with a little sense…'

'How?'

'Never thee mind about that now, there is much I must tell ye.
Now listen carefully:

'Now ye lay thee down to sleep,
Yon king and thee shall surely weep.
Quell thy darkness from this land,
Upon the pyre, hand in hand.
If ye find thy world lives on,
Live for dreams of Avalon.''

'What the hell does that mean?'

'Remember. Now take'th this goblet from me, walk into thy
darkness and drink heartily. It is as simple as that.'

'But its empty.'

'Think acrostically, my friend. When thy time is nigh, ye shalt
know what thou must do.'

'But what caused all this? What is the Darkness?

'In essence my friend, it is thee. It is contained within thee. It is the
darker thoughts and dreams of men that are not acted upon. I take
it that in thy realm ye are something of a bard, scribe or artist.
Would'st I be correct in mine assumption?'

'Yes, not a very successful one I grant you.'

'In the other realm, the king must walk in obscurity, he may draw
upon the darkness in his works, but he may never draw attention
upon himself. I'm sorry if this pains thee, but it is how it must be.'

'Okay… so why am I here?'

'Well basically, Avalon is sustained by the dreams of mortal men
in the other realm, thy realm in fact. The king, thy counterpart took
upon the burden of keeping the realms separate by remaining in
perpetual slumber, that his mind may bridge the gap between
reality and fantasy. But that said, he shalt remain a presence in
each to maintain his own dream-state. All creatures of myth and

legend that once existed in thy world came here to escape intolerance and extinction at the hands of a new and aggressive species.'

'Man?'

'Yes, ironic really isn't it that man shalt forever sustain that which he would slaughter without thought.' He chuckles.

'So what would happen to my world... realm if Avalon falls?'

'Could'st thou truly picture a world where humanity cannot dream? No inspiration, no art, no writing, no music. And what would become of humanity without its dreams and passions?'

'They would die of boredom'

'Exactly. So now me thinks ye understand the importance of thy success.'

'Yes, thank you for that, no pressure there then.'

'Thy flippancy does not become thee.'

'Yes, I've been hearing that a lot lately, stress reaction really.'

'Now, ye must act swiftly. I shalt hold back time and send thee to the threshold of thy darkness. Art thou ready?'

'As ready as I'll ever be'

'Then go, my friend, good luck and Godspeed to thee' he said with a wave of his hand.

The whole room disappeared from view and I was temporarily disorientated as I found myself stood before what looked like a huge black hole that destructively and violently consumed everything in its path. I'm suddenly pulled off my feet and forced headlong into the Darkness... My Darkness.

My counterpart king awaits me within and beckons me to him through the maelstrom. Like magnets we are drawn to each other. I hold the goblet aloft, but it is still empty.

'What is this? Did'st thee seek out 'the Ancient'?'

'Yes, he gave me this and said I would know what to do when the time comes'

'Well?'

'I don't know!'

'Art thou a half wit? What else did he say'eth to thee?'

'Hang on, there was a rhyme:

Now ye lay thee down to sleep,
Yon king and thee shall surely weep.
Quell thy darkness from this land,
Upon the pyre, hand in hand.
If ye find thy world lives on,
Live for dreams of Avalon.'

'What else did he say?'
'I'm thinking… think acrostically. That was it 'think acrostically''
'Then do so quickly'
'But what does it mean?'
'Thou truly art an imbecile, aren't thee? Acrostic poetry, thou
take'st the first letter of each line to form a word'
'Well now you've explained it… I still don't see how it helps'
'Try fool, before it become'th too late'
'N… Y… Q… U… I… L… Nyquil?'
'Nyquil? Is this some sorcery, magic or potion from whence ye
came?'
'I guess it is.'
'Behold, for thy cup runn'eth over.'
And it did, a huge dose of Nyquil filled the goblet.
'Kings before beggars my lord' I said and offered it to him. He
took it and drank heartily of the thick, green, pungent liquid, before
passing it back to me. I drank deeply, and my head began to spin.

I awoke, having sweated through the bed sheets, still feeling like
crap. Now, I've either just saved the world, two worlds in fact or
I'm still delirious from flu and Nyquil. I know which is the most
likely, but I also know which I'd prefer to believe.

Sweet dreams my friends……

The Body....

It all started at dawn, blurry eyed, yawning, plodding one foot in front of the other, feeling brain-dead, but looking like an extra from 'Shaun of the dead'.

I stumbled down the stairs on autopilot and switched on the kettle to assure my waking mind that its first caffeine fix of the day was imminent. As the kettle quickly rumbled to the boil, I rolled a cigarette to make my morning fix complete.

I lit the end of my nicotine pacifier and inhaled deeply of its glorious, deadly, cancerous pollen. And so my mind awakened to the prospect of another day. BOLLOCKS!!!

Coffee cup in hand, I stood and made my way to the sink and looked through the kitchen window to see what this new day offered and to my immense territorial outrage, I found some cheeky fucker sprawled out on my lawn embracing the morning sun.

So, arse firmly in my hand and preparing a tongue lash that could kill a man at ten paces, I unlocked the door. I stepped out into the dawn rays, squinting and shielding my eyes to investigate this dormant interloper. The closer I got, I realised that this stranger was not moving, at first I thought nothing of it and began proceed onwards. It was then that I saw there was no chest movement, no breathing and droplets of dew had collected around the face and clothes of this departed individual.

The coffee cup that I hadn't realised I was still holding, dropped from my hand in rhythm with my increasing heart beat almost in slow motion as the cup hit the ground and splashed its remaining contents over my bare foot before soaking into the surrounding soil. A chill played the length of my vertebrae like a skilled pianist, making the hairs on the back of my neck stand on end as the full gravity of my situation was realised. I didn't even notice, I had stopped walking when my coffee cup had hit the ground.

I was cautious, but I don't know why. Its not like the bastard was going to jump out at me, he's dead…..HE'S DEAD!!!!!

Arr, panic mode. I had to physically force myself forward to ascertain if my assumption was correct. Getting as close as I dared, I nudged him with my foot, fully expecting him to reach out and grab my ankle, thus releasing from me a high-pitched, girlish scream that would permanently crush my testosterone soaked ego. I released a sigh of relief as I realized that this is not to be the case, and knelt beside him to fully look death in the face.

I reached out and touched his cold clammy face, and was surprised to find his head did not move to the side as I had expected it too. His neck was stiff as a result of the blood pooling beneath him in rigour- mortis. I examined him and tried to bend his limbs as my panic gave way to morbid curiosity. Inappropriate thoughts began to fill my head as I pondered whether or not he was posable, and then further as I contemplated how I could pose this 'meat mannequin' in my garden amidst the gnomes, flowerbeds and hanging baskets.

My reverie was broken as a piecing scream shattered the dawn silence. I looked up and behind me, to find the location of this morning screamer. Ah, next door neighbour, top right bedroom window. Wide eyed, one hand covering her mouth while the other pointed at me as her husband joined her to see what all the noise was about. To my right was the freshly dug hole, I'd dug yesterday that was to be my new pond, and at the head of that was my spade, standing like a cross at the head of a grave. Realization dawned.

FUCK IT!!!!

And so began another day...

Madness & Murder...

The Room......

I return after so many years,
awaiting remembrance
to breach my lost past.
A cold unease consumes me,
as voices of forgotten ghosts
whisper softly to my senses...
Teasing my perceptions
with forsaken illusions...

Children playing, laughter,
music, the smell of fresh bread...
Such pleasant memories are these,
so why is my mind bestowing
this ill feeling dread upon me?
Numbness consumes my soul
from the very core of my being.
What happened here?

A scream, tearing flesh,
splash of blood, open wounds...
Moaning, hissing, crying... What is this?
Temples pounding... Racing heart,
fingernails digging into sweaty palms,
drawing bloody half moons...

The chair stands empty,
foreboding, familiar,
amidst unfolding memories
of lost dreams in an empty room...
Hooks, pain, blood, a cry...
Light bulb swinging, shadows swaying,
laughter, a voice... my voice...
my mind... my alter ego...

Welcome Home!!!

Death Art...

Day to day, finding prey,
To hunt when night doth fall.
Find the one, thy will be done,
And so my demons call.
Racing heart, a beat apart,
As lust for blood ensues.
So I crave, to misbehave,
The taste of fear, my muse.

So tonight, beneath lamp light,
Heels on concrete ring.
Hold my breath, for twilight death,
And all the pain I'll bring.
Now I stalk as prey doth walk,
Unknown to what's in store.
Looking round at every sound,
This primal fear so raw.

So turned on, I lust and long,
And strike from shadows cold.
Fearing eyes that question why,
Recoiling from my hold.
Fear thee not, thy fear begot,
The best is yet to come.
In my reign, I'll show you pain,
Before your senses numb.

In my heart, my work is art,
And she, my canvas bare.
Cut her deep, and make her weep,
And whimper as I stare.
Cutting lines as art defines,
With patterns crimson red,
Bleed her dry and bid goodbye,
Before her body's dead.

Passion quelled, where life once dwelled,
And now to bleach her skin.
Take away, my marks of play,
And wash away my sin.
Quickly ferried, corpse is buried,
Under basement floor.
So I weep, before I sleep,
And pray there are no more…

A Symphony of Dark Desires...

A divine symphony
of archaic pleasures
doth release the
Beast within…
Effervescent thoughts
disperse in dark clouds
behind mine eyes
as a veil of condensation
glazes my pupils…

I bite gleefully
into an over ripe plum
and wipe'th away
its rust coloured deposit
from my chin…

Mine heart-beat
doth quicken
as I does't see her,
consuming me
with a blood lust
that doth chill me
to my bones…

Unbidden thoughts
doth slither
amidst cascading
dreamscapes,
like a serpent in Eden…
Tempting me…
Taunting me…
Playing with me…

The evening's humid heat
overwhelms my senses…
I need air…

I need to think…
I need to dispel
these wrongful thoughts…
Why does't this virgin bride
fill'eth me with such
awful desires?

Its like a disease…
So primal…
So sexual in nature…
Would'st I truly sacrifice
everything in my life?
Just to let my demon rise
beneath a moonless sky
and sate his need?

He is very perceptive…
He awakens
and is lucid in my mind…
He softly whispers
his deviancy
to mine open ears,
causing me to blush
and salivate in rapture
at my moral decline…

He drives me…
Controls me like a machine
of most unholy intent…
And so I am lost…
Engulfed by my darkness
in a maelstrom of voices
as my very sanity ebbs
into a cold, empty void…
Beyond hope… Beyond reason…
Beyond salvation…

I smile to see that she has joined me…

<u>Someone Please Kill Me...</u>

Taking you to terror true,
unconscious from the street.
Keep you doped and tightly roped,
become my carnal treat.
Whimpered plea, 'Please don't hurt me'
I tell you, 'It's alright.'
I tape your mouth and journey south,
And consummate the night.

Grinding hips and fastened lips,
and grasping lady lumps.
Sawing limbs, while singing hymns,
as morphine numbs your stumps.
Flaying skin for what's within,
while keeping you alive.
I decree in blood-soaked glee,
'You'll live but won't survive.'

Carving flesh, so warm and fresh,
with herbs atop my shelf.
Roasting meat, so soft and sweet,
I feed you to yourself.
'Just stay calm, my lucky charm,
I do not wish you pain.
I have to feed this savage need
that's driving me insane.

No more sorrow, come tomorrow,
for you will cease to be.
I know its wrong, but oh so strong,
it haunts and tortures me.'
And so comes death, your final breath
as life fades from your eyes.
Left alone, my monster grown
becomes what I despise.

Please forgive this life I live,
for I have no control.
In too deep and losing sleep
as demons take their toll.
End me please, this sick disease,
just warps and twists my mind.
Make me stop, in death I'll drop
and leave this fiend behind.

Someone please kill me…

Temperance & Gluttony...

Refraining from female touch,
grinding teeth in carnal lust,
wanting what I cannot have...
Abstinence, my unseen foe,
my self-inflicted torment...
Its tearing me up inside,
rising the demon in me...

Such gluttony he brings me,
Craving flesh... to touch... to taste...
To hold... to have... to indulge...
I restrain him, he bites back...
His appetite grows stronger,
filling my mind with dark thoughts,
taunting me to act on them...

'No... I will not appease you...
Do you hear me? Never...'
His rage resounds to my core
I clench my hands to my head,
Temples pounding through fingers...
'Restrain... Restrain...' Tasting blood...
I bit my lip... It tastes good...

I felt pain... And... I liked it...
He laughs, drawing me to him
'Are we really so unlike?
Do you not feel it in you?
We are cut from the same cloth,
you and I, can you feel it?
We have so much work to do'

I shake, he terrifies me
and worse still, he may be right…
I try to suppress his voice,
but these urges… this blood lust…
It fills my mind… Such dark thoughts…
So all consuming… Help me…
I don't want to be evil…

My temperance, my demon,
Suppressing my desires
in exchange for craving flesh…
Please? This is not who I am…
Mincemeat, blue steak… not enough…
I cut myself to sustain,
never sating me… Need more!!!

Doorbell… Young girl from Greenpeace…
Please, come on in, my dear…
She kicks, she claws, she is lost…
Throat slit, pumping blood, wide eyes…
I gasp in sanguine rapture,
Smear her blood on my skin…
Devour her with relish

Pride in temperance, guilt in my gluttony…

In keeping with the theme of 7 deadly sins/7 heavenly virtues for a contest I entered, I created this form consisting of 7 verses, each with 7 lines, each with 7 syllables, ending with a line of 7 words... Oh & I nearly forgot the title has 7 syllables too

Having Friends for Dinner...

So very long, my endless song,
that sings throughout my days.
Bitter voices, full of choices,
how I count the ways.
So I crave, a friend to save,
my heart from all its sin.
So very lost, my soul the cost,
of darkness deep within.

I want to flee, so far and free,
beyond this lust inside.
That makes me kill, to feel the thrill,
appease my Mister Hyde.
I find my prey, upon this day,
a lamb in wait of slaughter.
So I hunt, my weapon blunt,
a blow that swiftly caught her.

Gagged and bound, without a sound,
she hangs on wooden beam.
Flay her hide, and woe betide,
her pain if she should scream.
Gleaming flesh, so warm and fresh,
as I pull on her pelt.
I wear her skin, to dance in sin,
where earlier she dwelt.

Such cold despise, in frightened eyes,
her sorrow drawing near.
No escape, is taking shape,
acceptance masking fear.
So concise, I slowly slice,
and carve her meat from bone.
Cutting deep, a sob, a weep,
so much I must atone.

So much pain, her blood I drain
and bleed her 'til she's dry.
In cutis coat, I slit her throat,
a gasp that questions why?
Cutting through, as organs spew,
I hollow out her shell.
My meaty treat, to later eat,
and book my place in Hell.

Further cutting, carving, gutting,
every morsel save.
Friend's who come, to sample some,
don't question what they crave.
Quickly season, within reason,
mince and chops and joints.
With each course, I lose remorse,
as nothing disappoints.

Boiling, roasting, lightly toasting,
savored kitchen smell.
Cooking meat, a nasal treat,
that makes one drool so well.
Would you care, to come and share?
I'll save a place for you.
Perfect dinner, for the sinner,
hides within you too.

You may think, my ethics stink,
but I'd just like to say.
When you eat lamb, or tender ham,
remember me this day.
Can't you see, you're just like me?
Your meat grunts, bleats or squawks.
And though mine, like yours is fine,
the difference is mine talks.

<u>God Complex...</u>

I may have been born of you,
but I am not one of you…
You sicken me, repulse me
with your abhorrent nature.
Self serving, paranoid,
territorial primitives,
serving the superficial,
worshipping the veneer
in vanity and self indulgence
in worthless lives
that amount to naught
but chaos in the turmoil of your flaws,
forever fighting in a world
that has not seen a day without war
since your creation…

I am the loner that does not fit in,
I am the truth that you ignore,
I am the conscience that you bury
in justification of your actions,
I am the justice from which you hide,
I am the darkness and the light,
I bring order to chaos,
I am the cure to this blight called humanity,
this scourge of the Earth's misery,
I am the man who would destroy the world…

And so I hear you laugh,
well lap it up my friend
'cause I'm top of the fucking food chain
and I'll be dabbing up your gravy
as I pick your chunks from my teeth.

You see, what you don't know doesn't hurt you,
blissful ignorance of imminent demise
allows you to carry on infesting
a dying world that begs its end.
And I will bring its end…

International waters, no law, no problem.
Your rules, your law, your game.
Drilling depths, punching crust,
penetrating layers of time
to drain a polluted ocean into a molten core,
building leagues of steam to fatal pressure
and so the planet tears itself apart.
You do the math, end of days,
End of the world,
Game over, Checkmate!!!
Eternity beckons…

You don't know
how long I've been doing it,
how close I am
or even if I've started.
Why don't you sleep on it
and tell me how you feel
in the morning,
if indeed
there is a morning…

Who's laughing now???

Strap my StraitJacket Tight...

When you lay me down to sleep,
ignore the tears I sadly weep.
Ignore the raging screams I cry,
ignore my shouts and questions why?
Ignore my eyes that plead to you,
ignore my Demon shining through.

Strap my jacket nice and tight,
Inject my meds to calm my night.
Ticking clock and gleaning sweat,
the twilight thoughts of lost regret.
Voices rage to fill my mind
and bleed into the shadows blind.

Taunting, tainting, makes me weak,
ignore seductive lies they speak.
Suppress my Demon breaking through,
beware the dreams he'll promise you.
Beware his words of honey gold
and watch his games and lies unfold.

Warped distortions to my eyes
in worlds that burn and all that dies.
See beyond the looking glass,
sibyllic dreams that come to pass.
I can but watch as futures change
and shift within my vision's range.

I can't affect the hand of fate,
events unfold and so I wait.
With but a touch, I'll see your heart
and know what tears your soul apart,
see your thoughts and life unfold
and know the secrets that you hold.

I don't feel safe to be around,
It's why I'm here so tightly bound.
Call me prophet, call me mad,
I'm lost in all the dreams I've had.
Kindly strap my jacket tight,
and bid to me a warm good night.

__Turbulent Clarity &__
__Perceptive Madness...__

Madness is but a perception
of illusions built
from the stones
of mortality…

For one man's insanity
is but another's vision
of turbulent clarity,
a prophecy etched
in the raw flesh
of a divine sojourn…

We are but products
of circumstance,
slaves to the past,
pushed to our limits,
punched through a veil
of chimera dreamscapes
to walk with
the specters and wraiths
that whisper in the shadows
of insomniatic preludes…

Living in the void
between ascendant thoughts,
holding back physicality
in choices made
in the breach
between moments,
a preemptive alacrity
of purpose,
heedless to consequence,
rippling the fabric of reality…

And so we wait as the world
finds affectation in our image,
holding the balance
between the Darkness
and the Light,
bound by Lithium chains
in claustrophobic cells
of Velcro restraints,
uncomprehending
to the minds
of rational falsehoods,
too tethered to actuality
to find purpose
beyond that which they touch…

But alas, visiting time is over
and though I'd so very much like you to stay with me...

...I also know…

…you're not really here…

www.ingramcontent.com/pod-product-compliance
Lightning Source LLC
LaVergne TN
LVHW091257080426
835510LV00007B/301